*The Fundamentals of*

# BRITISH MARITIME

# DOCTRINE

**BR 1806**

By Command of the Defence Council

DIRECTORATE OF NAVAL STAFF DUTIES
D/DNSD 8/36

LONDON: HMSO

ISBN 0 11 772470 X

*The Fundamentals of*

# BRITISH MARITIME

# DOCTRINE

BR 1'806

47064

# Foreword

By
**ADMIRAL SIR JOCK SLATER GCB, LVO, ADC**
*First Sea Lord and Chief of Naval Staff*

The British Isles are surrounded by sea and two thirds of the world is covered by water. Maritime power is thus of fundamental importance, both for national security and to support our world wide interests. Our geography and history have given us a uniquely powerful position at sea for a nation of our size. Therefore we must think clearly about the nature of maritime power and how it can be applied in support of the nation's foreign and security policies. This will enable us to fulfil our responsibilities at a time of great international change.

We in the Royal Navy must be careful to avoid a dogmatic approach in thinking about the principles that govern our maritime actions. We must maintain our reputation for innovation and for responding to political changes and technical opportunities. Yet there has always been a *doctrine*, an evolving set of principles, practices and procedures that has provided the basis for our actions. This doctrine has been laid out somewhat piecemeal in various publications and there has never been a single official unclassified book describing why and how we do our business. This publication aims to fill that gap by drawing together the fundamentals of maritime doctrine.

Doctrine draws on the lessons of history. So this book fuses historical experience with current thinking and terminology and I hope you will find this thought provoking. The drafting has been the work of a number of Naval officers and civilian historians and strategists in order to achieve a synthesis of experience and theory. To claim that the result is perfect would be nonsense. Indeed it would be contrary to the best traditions of the Service for any such codification of thinking to be regarded as unchallengeable. What follows has been accepted as doctrine by the Navy Board and thus represents an authoritative starting point for future debate. It is current doctrine which gives us all - both within the Service and beyond - a firmer idea of what we are about. It is thus a necessary foundation for the formulation of joint doctrine with the other Services. I expect this publication to be taught, applied, discussed and tested within the Naval Service and I commend it to all who have an interest in the profession of arms at sea.

Jock Slater

Admiral

# Contents

# Introduction

## Purpose

The purpose of this publication is to introduce the reader to the fundamentals of British maritime *doctrine*,[1] and to discuss its application in peace *crisis* and *war* in the context of the United Kingdom's foreign and security policy. This should be of deep professional interest to all Royal Naval and Royal Marines Officers and will have currency and relevance throughout an officer's career. Consequently on joining Britannia Royal Naval College officers should be introduced to the existence of the book and its content. They will be expected to be familiar with it on Initial Staff Course, and during other courses and appointments throughout their career. It should be made known to Warrant Officers on promotion and to appropriate Warfare Senior Ratings. It is also intended to be informative to a

1. Words in italics are defined or explained in the Glossary

### An Example of Successful Creation and Application of Doctrine

Nelson is well known for simple instructions such as his use of the signal "close action" - usually interpreted as "engage the enemy more closely" - and the sentence in his memorandum before Trafalgar that "No captain can do very wrong if he places his ship alongside that of an enemy." It is easy to be misled by the apparent simplicity of these instructions. In reality they reflected a confidence that his subordinates were completely familiar with contemporary Naval doctrine, amended sometimes by Nelson himself. Nelson, who was a great believer in delegation, expected his subordinates to use their intelligence, seamanship and understanding of his intentions to do much better in outmanoeuvering their opponents. Importantly, he devoted much time and effort discussing with his Captains how he pictured forthcoming battles. As a result, they were able to take independent action in support of Nelson's objectives without further reference to him.

**2.** Detailed operational, tactical and procedural doctrine is covered in The Fighting Instructions and associated publications.

**3.** When employed on military operations on land, the Royal Marines will take account of current land doctrine.

wider readership which includes the other Services, the Civil Service, Parliament, the academic community and the news media. As such, it aims to enhance appreciation of the contribution of maritime power to defence and security.

The Fundamentals of British Maritime Doctrine replaces The Naval War Manual, which contained the Royal Navy's previous statement of doctrine. The reference number of the earlier publication, BR 1806, has therefore been retained to demonstrate that doctrine is a longstanding concept for the Royal Navy not because of its proximity to the year of Trafalgar.

## The Role of Doctrine

Doctrine is a framework of principles, practices and proce-dures, understanding of which provides a basis for action. Maritime Doctrine fulfils this function for the use of mili-tary power at and from the sea to achieve policy objectives. It covers the *grand strategic, military strategic, operational* and *tactical* levels of military planning (defined in Chapter 2) both in *conflict* and in the peacetime applications of military power. This publication is concerned with the principles that govern the translation of national security and defence policy into maritime strategy, *campaigns* and operations.[2] It establishes a core understanding of the nature of maritime power both within and outside the Naval Service. Within the Royal Navy and Royal Marines[3] it provides a platform upon which all teaching, training and tactical de-velopment will build. Outside the Service it will generate wider understanding of the particular and distinctive nature of the maritime environment, and the ways in which *mari-time forces* operate. It will also serve as a source of considered advice for those charged with the formulation of Defence Policy, the Defence Programme and the procurement of military equipment.

## The Currency of Doctrine

Doctrine has its foundation in history; the study, analysis and interpretation of experience. It provides a shared interpretation of that experience which can be taught, in order to provide a common starting point for thinking about future action. This document sets out the current maritime doctrine of the Royal Navy and Royal Marines. Once written, doctrine can acquire a status that discourages change but it is important to prevent it becoming dogma. Doctrine must evolve as its political and strategic foundations alter, and in the light of new technology, the lessons of experience and the insights of operational analysis. This document should encourage discussion. It must not be a shackle on current thought but the springboard for future doctrinal evolution.

## Maritime Doctrine

This document is specifically concerned with the application of *maritime power*, as opposed to naval power. The difference is significant. Maritime power is inherently joint in nature. It emanates from forces drawn from all three Services, both sea and land based, supported by national and commercial resources, exercising influence over sea, land

### Maritime Doctrine

Sir Julian Corbett (1854 - 1922) provided the Royal Navy of the early Twentieth Century with its strategic doctrine. He set out clearly what doctrine was and what it was not. To Corbett, it was "not enough that a leader should have the ability to decide rightly; his subordinates must seize at once the full meaning of his decision and be able to express it with certainty in well-adjusted action. For this every man concerned must have been trained to think in the same plane; the chief's order must awake in every brain the same process of thought; his words must have the same meaning for all." At the higher strategic levels also there had to be a "common vehicle for expression and a common plane of thought." But Corbett always warned against slavishly following simple maxims and using them as substitutes for judgement. As he put it in his lectures; "You might as well try to plan a campaign by singing 'Rule Britannia'".

and air environments. Such influence has been greatly expanded with the advent of sea-based aircraft and missiles, the increased range of land based aircraft and modern techniques for amphibious warfare.

## Contribution to Joint and Combined Doctrine

All three British military Services contribute maritime forces, as do some non-military Services such as the Merchant Navy. Most major campaigns and operations will be *joint*; that is, they will involve forces of more than one Service and will frequently be combined, in conjunction with Allies.[4] This publication should therefore be considered as a contribution to both joint and combined doctrine. JSP 1 provides the fundamental tenets of United Kingdom Joint Doctrine and is aimed primarily at the staff of an *operational commander*. Army doctrine is described in The British Military Doctrine (Army Code 71451) while Royal Air Force doctrine is promulgated in Air Power Doctrine (AP 3000). Additionally, NATO provides its own Allied Joint Operations Doctrine in AJP 1A.

## Approach

The Fundamentals of British Maritime doctrine is designed to be read in the first instance as a logical progression from chapter to chapter. However, a reader who is broadly familiar with the subject matter but is investigating a specific topic will find that individual chapters stand on their own. Cross referencing has been used to minimize repetition. There is also a full Index and extensive Glossary for ease of consultation.

The book opens by outlining national security and defence policy, and the international framework of security organizations (Chapter 1). It then discusses general concepts governing the use of military force across the spectrum of conflict, and looks at the ways in which military force can be applied (Chapter 2). These early chapters are not specifically maritime in their approach but set the context for the remainder of the book. The maritime environment is first addressed in Chapter 3 where the distinctive features of the sea and the attributes of maritime power are introduced. Having set the scene, Chapter 4 examines specifically maritime doctrinal concepts, in particular *sea control* and *maritime power projection* and considers styles of warfare in the maritime environment. Chapter 5 covers the range of maritime tasks from the sea, at sea, and the policing and non-military tasks that are important functions particularly in peace. The focus then shifts specifically to the planning of campaigns and major operations. The general concepts that are introduced in Chapter 6 provide the link with other doctrinal publications such as *The Fighting Instructions and tactical publications.* Chapter 7 - Command and Control - includes a discussion of the particular qualities of leadership that are required at sea. Chapter 8 then addresses the important but often neglected subject of maritime *logistics.* The final chapter (Chapter 9) looks at the contributions of specific capabilities that a maritime commander will need to understand so that he can apply maritime doctrine in an operational environment. It concludes with a discussion of "the greatest single factor", the men and women charged with putting into practice the wide range of precepts, concepts, tenets and functions that earlier chapters have surveyed. The *Principles of War* are discussed at Annex A. The Falklands War of 1982 provides an excellent and comparatively recent illustration of the doctrinal principles expounded earlier. A short account, written from this viewpoint, is included at Annex B.

## Glossary

An important use of a book such as this is to provide a common strategic and operational language. For this reason many terms used in the text are printed in *italics* and defined in the Glossary. In some cases the Glossary lists more than one definition with an appropriate reference, however in some instances this is the first appearance in a Service publication of the definition.

# *One* 1

## Security and Defence Policy

*Doctrine* must be grounded in national security and defence policies. The former is concerned with risks to the independence and interests of a nation. These risks may be political, economic, social or environmental in nature, as well as military. Defence policy defines the military contribution to national security and is, therefore, a principal element of security policy.

1. Modified in 1954.

**Right:** RN SeaKing MK4
helicopter over
Bosnia in support
of UNPROFOR

# Introduction

The end of the Cold War has brought about profound changes in the security environment and a new pattern of global politics. Paradoxically, as superpower confrontation has eased, the comparative stability provided by previously accepted and clearly delineated spheres of influence has disappeared. The result is a less predictable world, posing new problems for all. Fortunately governments are now more aware of the damage that sustained violence can do to the global environment and economy, and of the need to address security concerns in a multinational context. This chapter will begin by considering the global and regional organizations that influence the United Kingdom before outlining UK security and defence policies themselves.

Most nations of the world are members of the UN whilst the Organization for Security and Co-operation in Europe (OSCE) [formerly the Conference for Security and Co-operation in Europe (CSCE)] includes in its membership most European countries as well as the United States, Canada and nations of the former Soviet Union. The Western European Union (WEU) and North Atlantic Treaty Organization (NATO) formed respectively by the modified Brussels Treaty (1948[1]) and the Washington Treaty (1949) are closely related historically and in their membership and functions.

# United Nations

The UN Charter stipulates that member states shall settle their international disputes by peaceful means, shall refrain from the threat or use of force against any state, and shall give the UN every assistance in any action which it takes in accordance with the Charter. Chapter V of the Charter governs UN *peacekeeping* operations and Chapter VIA enables the Security Council to determine the existence of any threat to the peace, breach of the peace or act of aggression, and to take such action by land, sea and air forces as may be necessary to maintain or restore international peace

and security. Article 51 of the Charter preserves the inherent right of individual or collective self defence if an armed attack occurs against a member of the UN.

During the Cold War, the UN was hindered from operating as the main guardian of international peace and stability. The executive functions of the UN Security Council were restricted by the hostility between East and West. However, since the end of sustained super-power confrontation, there has been greater consensus in the Security Council and an enhanced willingness for the UN to intervene in the troubled regions of the world, both in *conflicts* across borders and those contained within them. The UN's new significance in security affairs is reflected in the number of operations in which it has been involved recently. In the four decades up to 1985, the UN mounted a total of thirteen peacekeeping operations. Since then this figure has more than doubled and these operations have become increasingly complex and dangerous to the peace-keepers themselves. The UN has also authorized enforcement action by states or coalitions against threats to international peace

HMS VANGUARD
a nuclear powered
ballistic missile
submarine (SSBN)

and stability, notably against Iraq following the invasion of Kuwait in 1990 and in Somalia in 1992. The United Kingdom's responsibilities as a Permanent Member of the Security Council together with the capability of our armed forces has resulted in their use in an increasing number of these operations.

## North Atlantic Treaty Organisation (NATO)

NATO is the only multinational security organization with a structure of political consultation, assigned forces, integrated *command* and dedicated infrastructure and support. Member states of NATO also actively participate in other mutually supporting European security organizations, which include the Western European Union (WEU) and Organization for Security and the Co-operation in Europe (OSCE).

As the main threat to the security of individual members of NATO has changed, Alliance defence strategy has adapted. While the new environment has not altered the purpose of the Alliance - collective defence - it has provided an opportunity to adopt a broader approach to security. The Strategic Concept, published in November 1991, emphasizes effective crisis management and the further development of NATO's political dimension.

The 1991 Rome Summit's important initiative on dialogue and co-operation with Central and Eastern European (CEE) countries led to CEE Foreign Ministers meeting their NATO counterparts to form the North Atlantic Co-operation Council (NACC) in December 1991. The Council has continued to develop co-operation on specific security issues, including *peace support operations.*

Alliance decisions in 1992 to support peacekeeping operations under the authority of OSCE and UN were of profound significance in indicating NATO's willingness to use military measures beyond territorial defence. On 11 December 1992 the nations of the NATO *Integrated Military Structure (NIMS)* adopted peacekeeping as a NATO mission.

Royal Marines on peace
support operations

The 1994 Brussels Summit took a further important step in NATO's evolution in confirming that the security of its members is inseparably linked to that of all other states in Europe. It committed the Alliance to examine how current structures might be adapted, both to enable NATO to undertake the range of likely future missions more effectively, and to reflect the emergence of a European Security and Defence Identity (ESDI). The Summit launched three initiatives:

- The *Partnership for Peace* (PFP) programme to deepen political and military ties with CEE states, thus raising the possibility of the future expansion of NATO;

- The *Combined Joint Task Force* (CJTF) concept to enhance Alliance command arrangements and to permit a more efficient and flexible approach to Alliance missions. This concept is also intended for use in WEU operations and those involving non-NATO partners;

- Intensification of work to curb weapons proliferation.

## The European Pillar

The 1992 Maastricht Treaty established a European Common Foreign and Security Policy (CFSP) as a mechanism for governments of member nations of the European Union to co-ordinate European foreign and security policy. CFSP recognizes the need to develop a greater European responsibility for defence within the obligations of member states under the North Atlantic Treaty. The WEU is developing as the defence component of the EU and the European pillar of NATO. The Petersberg Declaration of WEU Ministers of June 1992 sets out a series of measures to strengthen the operational role of the WEU. It includes the identification of military units for use by the WEU when not required for NATO tasks, and the establishment of a WEU Planning Cell to prepare contingency plans. The Declaration also identified possible WEU missions in humanitarian operations, peacekeeping and crisis management fields; the so called Petersberg Tasks. These initiatives are complementary to NATO and as such consistent with the UK's approach: developing a European Security and defence Identity (ESDI) which should enhance the security and stability of Europe while recognising that NATO remains the enduring bedrock of any security architecture and avoiding unnecessary duplication. Command and forces for specifically European operations will be separable, but not separate, from NATO structures.

A multinational group replenishing at sea from a UK AOL

## Organization for Security and Co-operation in Europe

Nearly all European states belong to the OSCE making it the European security structure with the broadest membership. It provides a unique vehicle for promoting peace and stability in Europe. Since the 1992 Helsinki Summit, the OSCE has extended its role, taking on crisis management and peacekeeping tasks in addition to its traditional functions of developing confidence-building measures and arms control agreements. To give political legitimacy to its new role, the OSCE has become established as a regional organization of the UN.

## United Kingdom Security Policy

The United Kingdom's Security Policy is set in the context of the security organizations described above and illustrated at Figure 1.1. Its *aim* is to maintain the freedom and territorial integrity of the United Kingdom and its Dependent Territories and its ability to pursue legitimate interests at home and abroad. The collapse of the Warsaw Pact and the demise of the Soviet Union removed a direct and immediate military threat to the United Kingdom and her allies. Since 1991, the reduction of forces in Europe and the progressive establishment of mutual trust and co-operation between the West and its former adversaries has led to a greatly reduced risk of *general war.*

In the wake of these changes, however, new less well defined risks to the United Kingdom's security have emerged. Military force, together with other political and economic instruments, remains an integral part of any governmental response to security challenges. But the new strategic climate places demands on armed forces different from those of the Cold War period. British forces may often be used to prevent or limit conflicts as well as in the pursuit of broader national interests rather than defend territory. Although challenges within or close to Europe will be a primary security interest, the United Kingdom will need to maintain a capability for global reach and *power projection* to meet our obligations to the Dependent Territories and to protect and promote our world wide political and economic interests.

# United Kingdom Defence Policy

The 1995 *Statement on Defence Estimates* includes a public presentation of Defence Policy, which is a central component of wider security policy. It is expressed by means of three overlapping *Defence Roles* (DR) under which some fifty *Military Tasks* (MT) are grouped. The order of these roles does not reflect any priority between them although, in determining the level of resources and commitments, greater choice can be exercised in Roles 2 and 3 than Role 1. Defence Policy envisages seven general mission types that UK forces may be required to carry out in the execution of these Roles (See box below).

## Defence Role One

DR1 is to ensure protection and security of the United Kingdom and Dependent Territories even when there is no major external threat, which is self evidently the responsibility of any national government. The provision of an effective independent strategic and sub-strategic nuclear capability is a key DR1 task which also underpins British defence policy as a whole and is the ultimate guarantee of the country's

HMS NORFOLK
(Type 23) entering Cape
Town, South Africa

**2.** The titles of these catagories stictly reflect their function rather than their readiness. In origin they were designed to be components of a counter-concentration strategy against the now defunct Warsaw pact

security. Other DR1 tasks include the provision of military aid to the civil power in the United Kingdom and the reinforcement, if necessary, of British Dependent Territories.

## Defence Role Two

DR2 is to insure against any major external threat to the United Kingdom and our allies and is discharged through membership of NATO. NATO's force planning process for general war currently assesses that there would be sufficient warning time to regenerate and reconstitute forces to the required levels. The Alliance Strategic Concept published in November 1991 envisages flexible, mobile and multi-national forces. NATO *forces* are organized into *Reaction Forces* (RF), *Main Defence Forces* (MDF) and *Augmentation Forces* (AF)[2]. RFs and MDFs contain *Multinational NATO Maritime Forces (MNMF) and Area Forces.*

***Reaction Forces:*** forces at a high state of *readiness,* which in turn are divided into *Immediate Reaction Forces* (IRF) and *Rapid Reaction Forces* (RRF). Multinational Maritime IRF are

HMS ENDURANCE providing presence in the Antarctic.

formations continuously activated such as the NATO *Standing Naval Forces.* The Royal Navy has been contributing continuously to these standing naval forces since the commissioning of the Standing Naval Force Atlantic on 13 January 1968 at Portland Naval Base. RRFs are formations able to deploy quickly to a crisis area. *Maritime Multinational RRFs include NATO Task Groups (NTG), Task Forces (NTF)* and *Expanded Task Forces (NETF)*, which can all include amphibious forces.

*Main Defence Forces:* forces at a longer readiness than Reaction Forces but which would be made available for use when required. They provide units for the territorial defence of the Alliance. Many naval forces in this category are naturally at longer readiness in the cycle of maintenance and training. They can also provide a *roulement* of other forces at shorter readiness.

*Augmentation Forces:* units which will require significant time to become fully operational. For the Royal Navy augmentation forces consist of ships and submarines in refit, lengthy maintenance periods and those deliberately placed at extended readiness. Reserve personnel may assist in manning these units as their readiness is shortened.

*MNMFs* are NATO maritime forces organized into specific formations and intended to act as NATO's primary maritime crisis response forces.

*Area Forces* are those maritime forces committed to NATO, with the appropriate levels of readiness for RFs and MDFs, but not allocated to MNMFs. They may, however, operate in co-ordination with or in support of, MNMFs.

## Defence Role Three
DR3 is the promotion of the United Kingdom's wider security interests through the mainte-nance of international peace and security. Although the United Kingdom must retain a capability to act alone, operations under DR3 are

likely to be multinational, under the auspices of the UN, OSCE or WEU or as part of NATO or other coalition operations in support of UN or OSCE mandates.

## Seven mission Types for British Forces

**1** Military Aid to the Civil Power in the United Kingdom.

**2** A challenge to the internal or external security of a Dependent Territory.

**3** General war - a large scale attack against NATO.

**4** A limited regional conflict involving a NATO ally who calls for assistance under article 5 of the Washington Treaty.

**5** A British contribution to NATO's and the WEU's new missions.

**6** A serious conflict (but not an attack on NATO or one of its members) which, if unchecked, could adversely affect European security, or which could pose a serious threat to British interests elsewhere or international security.

**7** Other military assistance and limited operations, characteristically of lower intensity and longer duration, to support international order and humanitarian principles, most likely under United Nations auspices.

Source: Statement on the Defence Estimates 1995

# MEMBERSHIP OF INTERNATIONAL ORGANIZATIONS

As at 1 October 1995

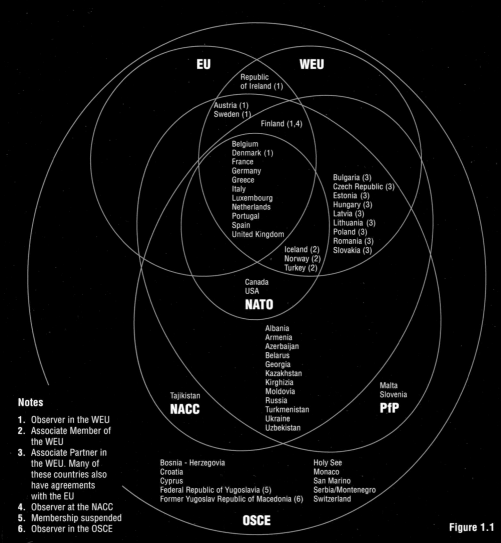

EU   WEU

Republic
of Ireland (1)

Austria (1)
Sweden (1)

Finland (1,4)

Belgium
Denmark (1)
France
Germany
Greece
Italy
Luxembourg
Netherlands
Portugal
Spain
United Kingdom

Bulgaria (3)
Czech Republic (3)
Estonia (3)
Hungary (3)
Latvia (3)
Lithuania (3)
Poland (3)
Romania (3)
Slovakia (3)

Iceland (2)
Norway (2)
Turkey (2)

Canada
USA

**NATO**

Albania
Armenia
Azerbaijan
Belarus
Georgia
Kazakhstan
Kirghizia
Moldovia
Russia
Turkmenistan
Ukraine
Uzbekistan

Tajikistan

**NACC**

Malta
Slovenia

**PfP**

Bosnia - Herzegovina
Croatia
Cyprus
Federal Republic of Yugoslavia (5)
Former Yugoslav Republic of Macedonia (6)

Holy See
Monaco
San Marino
Serbia/Montenegro
Switzerland

**OSCE**

## Notes

1. Observer in the WEU
2. Associate Member of the WEU
3. Associate Partner in the WEU. Many of these countries also have agreements with the EU
4. Observer at the NACC
5. Membership suspended
6. Observer in the OSCE

Figure 1.1

# *Two* 2

## General Concepts of Armed Conflict

To execute the Defence Roles discussed in Chapter 1 UK armed forces must be capable of operating from the extremes of violence typical of *general war* to at the other end of the scale, benign tasks in a stable peaceful environment. This chapter examines the general concepts governing the use of military force across this wide spectrum.

1. "Normal" levels of policing will vary from state to state.

2. Discrete or isolated acts of combat may take place outside hostilities.

## Violence and Conflict

In peace, nations in a normal state of economic competition with one another do not use *violence* to further their interests. If violence becomes a possibility in external relations, nations are said to be in *conflict*. If violence is threatened or used within a state's borders between competing groups for political reasons beyond levels that might be controlled by normal[1] civilian policing, that state is in *internal conflict*. The ways in which armed forces are used are governed by the presence or absence of conflict and the level of that conflict. The expression *Spectrum of Conflict* is often used to denote the full range of situations in which military forces may be called upon to operate, from stable peace to strategic nuclear war.

## Combat, Hostilities and War

*Combat* occurs at the higher end of the spectrum of conflict. Military combat is the organized use of violence by armed forces. Its purpose is to resolve conflicting interests by force in an attempt to achieve political objectives. In the period between the onset of regular combat and any cease-fire or truce, nations or groups may be said to be in a state of *hostilities*.[2] Combat that is intense, extensive and sustained over time may be termed *war.*

HMS SOUTHAMPTON (Type 42) firing a Seadart missile

## War

War is difficult to define simply. There is a legal definition that presumes a declaration of war and includes any period after declaration but before fighting begins. However, since 1964 there has been a reluctance formally to declare war largely because of the prescriptions of the United Nations Charter. There was, for instance, no declaration before the Vietnam, Iran-Iraq, Falklands or Gulf Wars. War is also very much a matter of the parties' perception. An insurgent may believe that he is at war, whereas the target government may consider the situation as one of peacetime disorder. In April 1982 the British public possibly believed themselves to be at war with Argentina, while the Argentinian government probably considered that they had achieved repossession as a fait accompli of gunboat diplomacy, which would be resolved by negotiations from a position of advantage.

The difficulty in defining war also applies to classifying types of conflict neatly as there are likely to be similar differences in perception between the protagonists of the scale of conflict and of the ends at stake. For example during the Vietnam War the Pentagon planners saw the conflict escalate from a counter-insurgency operation to limited war. To the Viet Cong guerrilla his fight for independence was always part of a general war against the government of South Vietnam and its allies. The Vietnam War also demonstrates how wars can frequently escalate in duration and intensity, as the momentum of conflict gathers pace despite the efforts by one or both sides to reduce forces and materiel levels in the theatre of war.

"War" meaning sustained, extensive and high intensity combat is, nevertheless, an important doctrinal concept. British Army Doctrine and US Navy Doctrine both distinguish between warfighting and Operations other than War (OOTW).

War in this sense does not lend itself to precise scientific analysis, in which causes can be related to calculable results. Instead war is a clash of wills with its own unpredictable dynamic, as actions, reactions, friction and the fog of war influence the scale, nature and outcome of combat.

RN fishery protection officer from HMS ORKNEY measuring the net size.

## How Military Forces are Used

Military forces can be used in three distinctly different ways which are labelled *military, constabulary* and *benign*. These modes of operation generally apply throughout the spectrum of conflict although military uses dominate the higher end when constabulary and benign activities will probably need protection by combat ready forces.

***Military (or Combat Governed) Use.*** A military use is one in which combat is used or threatened or which presupposes a combat capability. All warfighting tasks require the military use of force. Less obvious perhaps are the uses of military force in support of diplomacy discussed in Chapter 5 in which forces are used to coerce, persuade or signal a message. Although under these circumstances combat may not be used or even envisaged, it is the combat capability of the forces that underpins their use.

***Constabulary Use (Policing).*** Constabulary use is where forces are employed to enforce law or to implement some regime established by international mandate. Violence is only employed for self defence or as a last resort in the execution of the constabulary task. The ways in which force can be used will normally be prescribed in the law or mandate that is being enforced and there will be a general reluctance to employ violence. Combat is not, therefore, the means by which the mission is achieved even though the situation may warrant combat preparations, for instance for self defence.

***Benign Use.*** Benign tasks are those such as disaster relief, search and rescue or ordnance disposal. Military forces contribute organized and self-supporting formations with specific capabilities and specialist knowledge, for example *logistics* or civil engineering, but the tasks are benign because violence has no part to play in their execution.

However the mission of forces engaged in a particular *campaign* or *operation* may entail the use of force in more than one of these ways simultaneously or consecutively. For instance, benign disaster relief may require constabulary or military protection depending on the nature and scale of any threat (such as looting or attempts to exploit civic disorder to seize power). Similarly constabulary use may escalate into military use if there is a challenge of sufficient magnitude to the regime that is being enforced. For example, what may begin as Military Aid to the Civil Authorities, which is a constabulary task, may deteriorate into peace enforcement or evacuation operations, which are military or combat governed tasks. If disorder has deteriorated to extensive combat conducted by well armed groups or irregular forces, the task of restoring order will clearly be one requiring the military use of force. This is not to suggest however that these distinctions in the use of military force are in any sense arbitrary or a matter of degree. The legal basis for each of the three uses is different. Specific *doctrine* must be crafted for each use and a distinct attitude

A SeaKing (ASW) helicopter on a search and rescue mission.

**3.** The expression *attrition* is often loosely used as synonymous with destruction of denial. However *attrition* is also used more precisely to mean the wearing down of an opponent's ability to fight through destruction of his resources. This latter use is discussed more fully in Chapter 4.

**Right:** HMS VANGUARD (SSBN)

of mind is required of the command and military personnel involved.

Furthermore the perceptions of any potential or real opposition and of non-combatant civilians in theatre will to some extent decide whether a particular operation can be restricted to benign or constabulary use. As a result there are very real problems for military forces in a theatre in which forces ostensibly from the same nation, coalition or agency are simultaneously engaged in different uses of force. For instance it may be necessary for reasons of policy to carry out coercive tasks (military use) in the same theatre as the modest protection of a humanitarian operation (constabulary use). As a result any opposition might take the form of military reprisals against forces that are only undertaking constabulary and humanitarian tasks. UN operations in the Former Republic of Yugoslavia are an obvious example of these complexities.

## Ways in Which Military Force is Applied

*Destruction*[3] *and Coercion.* Military force may be used to destroy an opponent's military combat forces, his supporting logistics and military infrastructure, and under certain circumstances, non-military resources. Alternatively it may be used to threaten the destruction of items he values so as to *compel* him to abandon his objective. This is coercion. Destruction and coercion are concepts fundamental to the use of force in combat or its implied use in other situations. They are physical and psychological components of any military application of force and are therefore closely related. Destruction at one level of armed conflict may be coercion at another. Similarly limited destruction may be used to reinforce coercion. Conversely successful coercion may remove the need to resort to destruction. Coercion and destruction are also relevant to constabulary applications as enforcement relies on a measure of coercion. If coercion were to fail in a constabulary situation, there might be a need to resort to a measure of destruction. These two con-

cepts do not of course apply to benign uses.

*Disruption.* A third fundamental concept is that of disruption which brings together both physical (destructive) and psychological (coercive) components of the military use of force. Disruption of a military formation or combat system prevents it from functioning cohesively and, therefore, from performing successfully in combat. Disruption may be achieved physically by the destruction of elements essential to cohesion such as command, control, communications and information systems or *logistics*, or it may be achieved psychologically by affecting the decisions of the command and other individuals (for instance by surprise or *deception*), or by a combination of both.

## Deterrence

Force may also be threatened to help persuade an aggressor from resorting to combat in the first place. This form of coercion is *deterrence.* Deterrence is achieved when an opponent calculates that the potential costs of pursuing a particular course of action will outweigh the expected advantages to be gained. An opponent can be deterred through an assessment that:

- damage might be sustained to his military forces or to other valued resources from conventional or nuclear weapons (punishment);
- aggression will not succeed (denial).

## Nuclear Deterrence

Nuclear weapons have the potential to deliver a level of damage simply intolerable to any regime. Consequently their existence, and the impossibility of calculating at what stage in a conflict they might be used, can make it impossible for an aggressor to gamble rationally on achieving gains through aggression.

The ending of the Cold War has had the side effect of decrcreasing the potential for crises to develop to a level where nuclear weapons have relevance. Nevertheless, the Alliance's Strategic Concept clearly recognizes that, while conventional forces can ensure that no potential aggressor could contemplate quick or easy gains by conventional means, nuclear weapons make a unique contribution to war prevention. The United Kingdom's strategic nuclear capability continues to be the ultimate guardian of national security.

There are, however, circumstances in which nuclear deterrence would not be applicable. In a regional *crisis* which impinged on UK interests, a nuclear component to deterrence might be affected by security assurances which the UK - like other Nuclear Weapon States - has given. Moreover nuclear deterrence might be simply dis-proportionate to the situation and therefore lack credibility. The collapse of the Soviet bloc and the subsequent disintegration of the Soviet Union itself have greatly reduced the possibility that a regional conflict might escalate into a confrontation between the superpowers. It has also, however, removed some restraints on nations seeking to achieve their regional objectives by military means.

## Conventional Deterrence

The worldwide resurgence of nationalism and religious extremism has made it more likely that force will be used to resolve disputes between states. The consequent instability remains of concern to the United Kingdom creating potential for our armed forces to get involved in regional disputes, either as part of an international coalition or as a national operation. Our conventional forces will therefore continue to provide a measure of deterrence in situations in which nuclear deterrence is not feasible or appropriate. Deterrence might be achieved through a capability to launch accurate conventional attacks against objects of high value to a potential aggressor government. Alternatively, demonstrating a capability to intervene or reinforce by placing *maritime forces* in the vicinity of a threatened ally might

HM Ships
NORFOLK (Type 23),
BOXER (Type 22) and
NEWCASTLE (Type 42)

demonstrate to the potential aggressor either unacceptable likely costs of aggression or the probability that it would not succeed. Essential to effective military deterrence is political and military credibility which in turn are built on a history of resolute policy and of military effectiveness.

## Legality of Conflict

The laws of armed conflict are international law. As such they are in part derived from treaties that have been made between states and, in part "customary" law, which has developed over time from the widely accepted practice of states. Treaty based law is only binding in conflicts between those States who are signatories to the relevant treaty. However, most States are parties to the most substantial and widely applicable sets of treaty provisions, namely the Charter of the United Nations (1945), the Hague Conventions, (1889 and 1907) and the Geneva Conventions (1949).

There are two categories of laws of armed conflict: jus ad bellum, which is law governing the occasions on which force may be legally used; and jus in bello, which is law that seeks to regulate the actual conduct of hostilities.

With regard to jus ad bellum, the UN Charter prohibits the threat or use of force against the territorial integrity or political independence of any State [Article 2(4)], but permits the inherent right of individual or collective self defence [Article 51]. For this reason the requirement for a UN mandate has increasingly been considered a prerequisite for intervention or enforcement action. While the decision to engage in armed conflict is political, the issue of self defence is of great concern to military commanders who are responsible for the protection of their forces.

For jus in bello, the Geneva Conventions seek to protect the victims of armed conflict: wounded, sick, prisoners of war and civilians. The Hague Conventions regulate the means and methods of warfare and include rules governing:

- combatant status, which is the right of uniformed military forces to participate in hostilities;

- what constitutes a legitimate target - attack on a civilian population and civilian targets is forbidden (the principle of distinction), and collateral civilian casualties and damage must not be excessive in proportion to the expected military advantage (the principle of proportionality);

- categories of weapon that may not be used, specifically those that cause unnecessary suffering (unnecessary suffering principle), those that cannot discriminate between military and civilian targets (discrimination principle), and certain categories of "treacherous" weapons (treachery principle).

Specifically maritime provisions of International Law are covered in Chapter 3. The concept of national and multinational Rules of Engagement (ROE) crafted to control the use of military force for specific operations is described at Chapter 7.

**4.** In Figure 7-1 in the chapter on Command and Control these levels are related to the levels of command in the United Kingdom joint command structure.

**5.** The expressions "strategic", "operational" and "tactical" each have a number of meanings and are also frequently used loosely and in a broader sense than a specific level of command and planning. For instance *OPCOM/OPCON* and *TACOM/TACON* have precise definitions that do not necessarily relate to the Operational or Tactical Level of Command (See Glossary)

# Levels of Command and Planning for Military Operations (The Levels of War)

Traditionally military operations have been planned at four levels which are outlined in the box below[4]. These levels of planning apply to all types of conflict at all levels of intensity. The distinctions between the levels of command and planning are not precise, especially in the maritime context. In general terms, the larger the conflict the more hierarchical are the *levels of war*. In conditions of global conflict there would be clear differences between the four levels. In more limited conflict single engagements may be decisive and so local tactical factors can assume military strategic significance[5]. Figure 2.1 at the end of this chapter relates each level to common expressions for the scale of military activity at that level.

## Levels of Command and Planning for Armed Conflict (The Levels of War)

**Grand Strategic.** The level of command and planning for armed conflict (level of war) at which all the resources of a nation or multinational coalition (diplomatic, economic, military, political, informational and technological) are applied to achieve national security or coalition policy objectives. Grand strategic decisions are generally taken by governments or, in a coalition, agreed between governments.

**Example:** the decision taken by the British Government to re-establish sovereignty of the Falkland Islands in 1982 was a decision taken at the grand strategic level.

**Military Strategic.** That component of national or multinational strategy, representing the manner in which military power should be developed and applied to achieve national objectives or those of a group of nations. It is the application of military resources to achieve grand strategic objectives.

**Example:** the decision to use submarine and carrier/amphibious task forces first to coerce the Argentines to withdraw and subsequently to retake the islands was one taken at the military strategic level.

**Operational.** The level of command and planning for military operations (level of war) at which campaigns and major operations are planned, conducted, and sustained to accomplish strategic objectives within theatres or areas of operation. The orchestration of military activities at this level is termed operational art and provides the crucial link between the setting of military strategic objectives and the tactical employment of forces. At the operational level planning and execution are usually joint and often combined.

**Example:** the decisions on where to deploy the carrier battle group in relation to the islands and where and when and with what forces to make the amphibious landings were operational.

**Tactical.** The tactical level of warfare involves the direction of military resources to achieve operational objectives. The role of the tactical commander is to ensure the most effective use of units under his command or control.

**Example:** the disposition of the escorts in relation to the carriers in the battle group was a tactical decision

## Types of Armed Conflict

*General and Limited War.* Armed conflict may take the form of general war, a conflict with few restrictions, involving all the resources of a nation. Alternatively it might be a *limited war*, that is, sustained hostilities which may be limited significantly in area, in the means and methods used, in the time available to bring them to a successful conclusion and in the political objectives at stake.

*Intervention.* Where the somewhat hazy criteria for war discussed in the box on page 33 are not considered to apply, operations which involve entering the territory or other areas of jurisdiction of other states where opposition is expected, are *interventions*. An armed intervention is one during which armed combat is used, threatened or envisaged. *Peace enforcement,* which is in itself a form of armed intervention, is discussed in more detail in Chapter 5.

***Insurgency and Counter-Insurgency.*** Campaigns within the borders of a state to overthrow or restrict the authority of a government are *insurgencies*. The use of military forces against insurgents is *counter-insurgency*, a problematic form of conflict in which solutions will be political rather than military. Armed forces may well be expected to perform an awkward combination of constabulary and military tasks. There is not a clear distinction between an insurgency and civil war. Indeed civil war may be a phase of successful insurgency. Generally in a civil war the population is itself divided into two or more factions which seek either to control the government or to achieve independence or autonomy for a region. *Counter-terrorism* is a campaign principally for specialist forces. However regular forces may be required to provide support in the form of constabulary tasks and, occasionally, specifically military functions.

## Escalation

Whenever armed forces are employed in conflicts, there is a risk of *escalation*. If the situation worsens, forces must either be capable of higher intensity operations, withdraw or face defeat. If forces find themselves in situations involving potential or actual combat on a larger scale, of greater intensity or longer duration than that for which they were prepared, this is known as *embroilment*.

Escalation can be *vertical* or *horizontal*. Vertical escalation is an increase in the level of violence (in quantity, or by the introduction of new categories of weapon such as chemical or nuclear weapons, or indeed by the inclusion of target sets that had hitherto been spared[6]). Horizontal escalation is the extension of combat geographically to new theatres or environments.

Escalation may be the deliberate choice of one side which has the resources to use overwhelming force to minimize risk, or whose initial campaign plan has bogged down, or which risks defeat as the situation stands. It may also be the result of expanding *war aims*, perhaps to justify or compensate for expenditure to date. Escalation may also be an involuntary spiral. As such it is one of the factors that makes the outcome of war unpredictable.

**7.** See footnote 3 on page 36 for a discussion of *attrition*

A similar concept to escalation, and one that may be favoured by a weaker side, is the deliberate *prolonging* of a campaign to exhaust a protagonist or wear down resolve by some combination of *attrition*[7], expenditure of resources and internal political capital.

The threat or the use of weapons of mass destruction (WMD) would lead to an immediate re-evaluation of the limitations of any armed conflict. In the Gulf War (1990-91) US Secretary of State James Baker alluded to the possible consequences of escalation when he implied that use of WMD by Iraq against coalition forces would result in a change in Coalition political objectives to include the over-throw of Saddam Hussein.

## Principles of War

The application of military force at the military strategic and operational levels is both science and art. Essential to the art of a military leader is the ability to learn from his

RFA Sir TRISTRAM (LSL) off loading with HMS FEARLESS (LPD) in the background

own experience and that of others. The *Principles of War* are
a distillation of experience and a simplification of complex
and sometimes contradictory ideas. They are broad precepts for the conduct of armed conflict. They should be
used to inform all military strategic and operational decisions rather than as a planning checklist. The ten Principles
recognized by the armed forces of the United Kingdom are
listed in the box below and explained at Annex A.

### The United Kingdom Principles of War

Selection and  Maintenance of the Aim

Maintenance of Morale

Offensive Action

Surprise

Security

Concentration of Force

Economy of Effort

Flexibility

Cooperation

Administration

# HIERARCHY OF MILITARY ACTIVITY

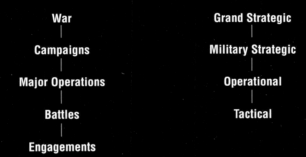

| MILITARY ACTIVITY | LEVELS OF WAR |
|:---:|:---:|
| War | Grand Strategic |
| Campaigns | Military Strategic |
| Major Operations | Operational |
| Battles | Tactical |
| Engagements | |

Figure 2.1

# *Three* 3

## The Maritime Environment and the Nature of Maritime Power

Maritime *doctrine* is concerned specifically with the application of maritime power at sea and *maritime power projection* from the sea. This chapter examines features of the maritime environment and the nature and attributes of maritime power.

1. The equivalent colloquial expression for coastal and inshore waters is brown water but this is a misleading term as it implies conditions such as shallow water that do not necessarily prevail in *littoral* waters. Green water is occasionally used to mean continental shelf waters.

# Environmental Factors

The maritime environment influences the way in which maritime forces can achieve their objectives.

*Coverage.* Seventy percent of the Earth's surface is covered by the sea, providing a medium for the efficient transport of large and bulky items.

*Resources.* The sea is increasingly being exploited for the economic resources it holds and covers.

*Access.* Approximately seventy percent of the world's population lives within one hundred miles of a coastline. The sea thus gives vital strategic *access* to the centres of population and therefore to governments.

*The Physical Environment.* Operating areas for maritime forces vary from open oceans and great seas, known colloquially as blue water, to the more confined waters[1] of *littoral* regions, estuaries and rivers. A good knowledge of the physical environment in which maritime forces are to operate is essential. Geographic, oceanographic and meteorological conditions will affect the ability of maritime forces to conduct operations. The effect of high sea states on flying

HMS HERALD
Ocean Survey Ship
off Portland

operations and sonar performance are examples. These conditions will also affect an enemy. However, skilful seamanship and well rehearsed tactics and procedures can reduce these effects. Adverse conditions can also be used to advantage; a submarine for example can use poor sonar conditions to avoid detection. The mobility of maritime forces may allow them to move to an operating area where conditions are more favourable. A carrier can, for instance, seek out and exploit a local window in poor visibility to continue flying operations. Expertise in oceanography and meteorology and comprehensive hydrographic support must be available to a commander if he is to exploit the maritime environment fully and minimize its adverse effects.

*International law.* Considerations of international maritime law and the law of armed *conflict* (see Chapter 2) will always affect the freedom of action of a commander at sea. In the broadest terms, these considerations are:

- Operations may not be conducted in the *territorial seas* or *archipelagic waters* of neutral states, that is states not party to the conflict.

- Although warships may generally exercise the right of *innocent passage* through the territorial or archipelagic waters of neutral states, while so doing they may not operate aircraft (except for search and rescue), weapons systems or certain sensors. These restrictions do not apply while in transit through *international straits.*

- Within the *Exclusive Economic Zones* of states that are neutral in a conflict, due regard must be paid by military commanders to the rights of the coastal state.

- Due regard must also be paid by belligerent commanders to the natural environment.

*Freedom of the Seas.* As indicated above, International Law provides legal access for ships up to the territorial seas of

HMS TRAFALGAR (SSN)
a SeaKing MK 6 (ASW)
helicopter

**2.** 92% by volume and 76% by value of the United Kingdom's trade moves by sea (Statement on the Defence Estimates 1995)

nations and rights of innocent passage for the purpose of either traversing territorial waters without entering *internal waters*, or proceeding in either direction between the high seas and internal waters. A passage is innocent provided that it is not 'prejudicial to the peace, good order or security of the coastal state'. Given this caveat, access is unrestricted. Thus, *maritime forces* can approach and pass through the territorial waters of a nation legally and without prior approval of the government concerned. If, therefore, their posture and activities within territorial waters are lawful, they have considerable freedom of movement. However care must be taken by forces poising off a coast not to infringe the territorial rights of the coastal state.

**Trade.** Most of the United Kingdom's[2] trade and much of that of the European Union is moved by sea. Our economy and those of our European partners are vulnerable to large scale interference to shipping. By the same token trade *sanctions* and *embargo* are useful diplomatic tools which maritime forces may be required to implement. Increasingly maritime trade is becoming supranational. Ships belonging to a company registered in one nation may be registered under the flag of another with crews from yet others. Additionally shipping companies themselves may be parts of international conglomerates as may the owners of the cargo being carried. Thus, responsibility for protection of shipping and the interest in its safety are increasingly complex matters.

*Military Challenges.* Maritime forces continue to expand in numbers and capability in many parts of the world, notably in the states around the Arabian Gulf and the Asia/Pacific rim. The adjacent seas carry a large amount of trade which is critical to Western economic prosperity.

## The Multidimensional Maritime Battlespace

Maritime forces must be capable of operating above, on and below the surface of the sea. The oceans provide three dimensional space in which maritime forces can operate and manoeuvre, and an international arena for the demonstration of capability and the will to use force. However, a threat can come from any direction and an enemy's position and movement must be established through three dimensional surveillance. All systems, including space and air based area sensors, must be used to maintain a continuous and timely flow of information. The sea is, however, largely opaque to many sensors. It can therefore be used as a hiding place, for example for *strategic nuclear deterrent* patrols by ballistic missile firing submarines.

Surface ships are vulnerable to detection by satellite or air surveillance but it is often hard to locate and identify targets with sufficient certainty to engage them, especially if they are not radiating. In open waters, attacking forces will usually have wide options for a direction of approach and may pose an all round threat placing large demands on defending forces. This factor will tend to favour the offensive, though defending forces can concentrate strength around units at risk. The possibility of drawing the attacker to his destruction in certain circumstances can redress the balance in favour of the defensive. Indeed an engagement might be positively welcome in providing an opportunity to inflict attrition on the enemy.

The proximity of land places limitations on freedom of movement, avenues of approach and both offensive and defensive options. There may be no alternative to passing through geographic choke points or waters in which detection is difficult and the possibility of surprise attack enhanced. The littoral environment will generally favour forces that can exploit limited warning time to their advantage. Surveillance and weapon systems must be capable of dealing with the more cluttered coastal region and detecting attackers over land. Maritime forces must be capable of operating equally well in both open ocean and littoral regions of the world.

## The Nature of Maritime Power

Maritime power in the broadest of sense is military, political and economic power exerted through an ability to use the sea. Maritime power has traditionally been employed to control sea communications for the general economic welfare or survival of sea dependent states. Military maritime power has also had a longstanding ability to influence events on land through amphibious and ship launched land attack operations. This power projection capability has greatly expanded with the advent of modern amphibious techniques and the advent of sea based aircraft and land attack missiles. Thus while maritime power has seaborne air and land fighting from the sea components, the unifying factor is use of the sea. This aspect is covered more fully in Chapter 9.

Professor Gray (see box) has drawn two general truths from his study of the use of maritime power throughout history. First, a continental power can win a war if it is able to secure military command at sea, achieve *sea denial*, or even just dispute command at sea very vigorously. Secondly, for a sea power or a maritime-dependent coalition,

## The Impact of Maritime Power

In the prologue to his book "The Leverage of Seapower" Professor Colin Gray sets out the impact of maritime power in these words:

"....[it] grants the ability to control the geostrategic terms of engagement in war. Depending on who controls the sea, water is a highway or a barrier. The continuity of the world's seas and oceans translates into a global mobility and agility for maritime forces which can have no continental parallel. That mobility and agility has been used time and again, in all historical periods to achieve surprise and the full strategic advantage of surprise effect. Finally, and notwithstanding the several revolutions in transportation technologies for all environments over the centuries, superior seapower has enabled its owners to knit together coalitions with a total strategic weight greatly superior to those secured by dominant continental strength". (Copyright© 1992 by Colin S Gray)

In his classic expression of British Maritime Doctrine, "Some Principles of Maritime Strategy" (1911) Sir Julian Corbett explained the limits of naval and, by implication, maritime power. He argued that it was:

"almost impossible that a war can be decided by naval action alone. Unaided, naval pressure can only work by a process of exhaustion. Its effects must always be slow, and so galling both to our own commercial community and to neutrals, that the tendency is always to accept terms of peace that are far from conclusive. For a firm decision a quicker and more drastic form of pressure is required. Since men live upon the land, and not upon the sea, great issues between nations at war have always been decided - except in the rarest of cases - either by what your army can do against your enemy's territory or else by the fear of what the fleet makes it possible for your army to do".

HMS BOXER (Type 22)

command at sea provides the strategic conditions indispensable for success in war. These propositions explain the strategic dependency of both the United Kingdom and NATO on maritime power.

The maritime power that a maritime nation and alliance requires for security in the event of major attack can be used to protect national interests in situations of lesser conflict. It can also provide opportunities to contribute to wider security and stability through conflict prevention and *conflict control.*

The utility of maritime forces is most evident when they form part of a *joint expeditionary* force in the execution of a strategy designed to achieve objectives ashore by using *access* from the sea as a principal factor. Land forces may only be able to obtain access if they are landed by *naval forces* in amphibious operations. Even when this is not the case, ground forces may be prevented from achieving their objectives unless maritime forces can safeguard their *lines of support.*

***The Balance of Risk at Sea.*** Movement of naval forces on the high seas can take place without prior diplomatic agreement. Furthermore combat in open waters does not violate territorial integrity nor entail much risk of *collateral damage* to innocent parties. Maritime operations may therefore be conducted under conditions of greater political risk than land operations. On the other hand a maritime force may include valuable units and there may be important political, psychological, and operational consequences, if these are subject to *catastrophic* damage. The management of military risk is therefore an important element of any operation. The relatively unconstrained use of the seas allows the commander to manage risk to his force through choice of route and environment, and ease of extrication. In littoral waters, however, his options are likely to be more restricted. A warship corresponds in political and military significance to a substantial ground or air formation. and its loss would be correspondingly more significant than that of a single air-craft or tank. However a warship is resilient and has other attributes discussed in the next section which greatly reduce the probability of loss.

## Attributes of Maritime Power

Success in a major operation will usually require the partici-pation of sea, land and air forces. Individual military units need to co-operate and complement each other to achieve the common aim. Maritime forces bring the following operational attributes.

*Mobility.* Maritime forces can move hundreds of miles per day over more than two thirds of the world's surface. Mobil-ity enables maritime forces to respond from over the horizon, becoming selectively visible and threatening to ad-versaries, as needed.

*Versatility.* Warships can easily change their military posture, undertake several tasks concurrently and be rapidly avail-

BV 206 All Terrain Carrier coming ashore from a Landing Craft Utility (LCU)

**3.** A concept broached by Rear Admiral J R Hill in "Maritime Strategy for Medium Powers"

able for others. They can present a range of flexible and well calibrated political signals. Furthermore naval command, control and information systems (CCIS) at the strategic, operational and tactical levels offer uniquely controllable forces to complement diplomacy. There is, however, a corollary to versatility in support of diplomacy. Those being signalled may misunderstand the level of threat being posed, and concurrent diplomatic activity may be required to resolve unintended ambiguity. The elements of versatility can be summarised as:

*Flexibility in response.* Ships at high *readiness* are manned and provisioned for hostilities and their systems and crews can rapidly respond to contingencies by progressing quickly from peacetime cruising to a more combatant posture if required.

*Adaptability in roles.* An individual warship of frigate size and above will have defensive capabilities in all three dimensions (air, surface and sub-surface) and offensive capabilities in one or two. It can therefore operate in a variety of operational environments. Warships can be formed into *task forces and groups* (which may be multinational) where their individual characteristics combine to provide a mutually supportive suite of offensive and defensive capabilities. This allows the group to operate at higher threat levels where conditions would be beyond the capability of a single ship. A task force or group possesses an array of surface, air and subsurface assets that operate as a whole. Modern warships can therefore be as much parts of an overall system as they are individual units.

*Sustained Reach.*[3] Naval forces have integral *logistic* support, including repair and medical facilities. The range and *endurance* that these provide, give individual maritime units sustained *reach*, that is the ability to operate for extended periods at considerable distance from shore support. *Reach*

HMS NEWCASTLE
(Type 42)

is enhanced by the provision of *organic* and *consolidation* tankers, supply and repair vessels. Only a navy so equipped can exploit the full potential of maritime power. If reach is to be sustained for an extended period, a *roulement* of replacement forces may be required. (See Chapter 8). Seaborne logistic support is an important element in sustaining joint operations.

**Resilience.** Warships are designed to absorb substantial damage before they become non-operational. While a loss of capability through damage will degrade operational performance, a ship is designed with this in mind and her company trained to restore equipments to use as quickly as possible. They are also designed to operate within areas contaminated through the use of WMD without degradation to their operational capability.

**Lift Capacity.** *Sealift* allows amphibious forces to transit to and poise in theatre, and then enables maritime power to be brought to bear ashore. Furthermore it may often be the only practicable means of deploying significant land and air forces, their battle winning equipment and logistic support, into a joint theatre of operations quickly and cheaply. As Britain is an island, all major operations necessitate some maritime support to deploy, resupply, withdraw, or redeploy the units involved. Although the *Royal Fleet Auxiliary* provides some sealift, a major operation relies for *lift* on merchant shipping, which may not necessarily be British. An important duty for maritime forces is protecting the free passage of this sealift.

*Poise.* Once in theatre, maritime forces can remain on station for prolonged periods, either covertly or more openly. They can keep options open or signal political resolve, and act as a force for *deterrence* or active *coercion*. The ability of maritime forces to poise in international waters avoids the political complications and military risks of deploying forces on land. Maritime forces can be withdrawn without the stigma of retreat. This unique capability to match the pace and reflect the tone of diplomatic activity is particularly useful in the confused and uncertain situations of the post-Cold War world. Poise exploits mobility, versatility, sustained reach, and lift capacity. (See Chapter 5 on the use of naval forces in support of diplomacy).

*Leverage.* Through suitable positioning maritime forces can provide maritime *leverage*, to exploit access and have an effect on events occurring on land disproportionately greater than the scale of maritime force applied. Leverage is both a strategic and an operational concept. Its effects can be directly political or primarily military. Leverage for political effects involves the coercion of governments which, outside *hostilities*, is an aspect of naval diplomacy (See Chapter 5). By way of military example, at the strategic level a maritime nation or coalition can use maritime and other expeditionary forces skilfully to shape the war ashore, to prevent concentrations of enemy force on vulnerable fronts, or in decisive *campaigns*. At the operational level amphibious and

A Nimrod maritime
patrol aircraft flying over
Royal Navy and United
States Navy submarines at
the North Pole

other naval forces on a seaward flank can provide *manoeuvre from the sea* to *distract* and tie down much larger forces ashore or to *envelop* or otherwise achieve the *disruption* of larger forces ashore.

***Joint Attributes.*** Navies have traditionally taken part in operations involving other services and, through providing amphibious capability, regularly practise what could be considered the ultimate joint operation. Maritime operations are joint by definition as they involve forces operating both afloat and ashore - and nowadays in the air. Naval forces can provide afloat headquarters for joint forces offering advantages in flexibility and access. In a phased campaign there may be a requirement for a joint command to be afloat initially and subsequently move ashore - and vice versa during a withdrawal, redeployment or evacuation. With its amphibious component a maritime force makes an all arms contribution to joint operations.

*Combined Attributes.* British maritime forces are made up of discrete national units well practised in operating in multi-national groups, either within NATO or in ad hoc coalitions. Inherent mobility allow maritime forces to assemble easily and the use of NATO procedures allows multinational groups to be effective with a minimum of planning and preparation. If combat is a possibility, however, multinational maritime forces benefit from prior periods in company to exercise and develop their full operational effectiveness.

## Additional Factors

*Intelligence and External Information Support.* Modern communications systems provide maritime forces with quick and comprehensive access to an enormous amount of information and intelligence drawn from a wide range of sources, many of which are external to the ship or force. Coupled with the available organic sensors and data handling systems, communications and information systems give maritime forces unprecedented capacities to compile an accurate picture of their operational and tactical environment. Communications also enhance the synergy between all systems in space, in the air, ashore, afloat and below the surface of the sea.

*Cost-Effectiveness.* While seemingly expensive in terms of procurement, training and shore-based infrastructure, warships are more than mere "weapon platforms". They are integrated command, sensor and weapon systems, interfacing with other forces to provide a uniquely versatile package of capabilities. It is difficult, therefore, to compare the cost-effectiveness of a warship with another type of unit or formation whose range of roles is narrower. Once operational a warship can be deployed and employed extensively with modest additional logistic cost.

*Life Cycle.* A ship takes time to build and is designed for a long operational life. There must therefore be planned opportunities to update individual sensors and systems as required. By this means ships can be maintained at high levels of operational capability, even in an era of rapid technological progress.

## Conclusion

The potential and relevance of maritime power in today's world is as great as ever. Maritime forces operate in an environment that allows them access to most potential *crisis* areas of concern to the United Kingdom and our Allies. Maritime forces are mobile, versatile and resilient, and can contribute sustained reach and lift capacity to a joint campaign or operation. Their ability to poise makes them powerful tools of diplomacy, and a capacity for leverage particularly in the context of expeditionary operations is of greater importance than ever in today's world of risks and uncertainties.

### Principal Attributes of Maritime Forces

Mobility

Versatility

Sustained Reach

Resilience

Life Capacity

Poise

Leverage

# *Four* 4

## Concepts Governing the use of Maritime Power

Chapter 2 described the ways in which military forces can be used. These can be categorized usefully as *military* (or *combat governed*), constabulary (or *policing*) and *benign* uses. The general concepts discussed in this chapter are those specifically relevant to the military or combat governed applications of maritime power at the strategic, operational and tactical levels. As Chapter 5 will make clear, combat governed tasks are not confined to *hostilities* but are applicable across the whole *spectrum of conflict*.

To use the sea a nation must have sufficient freedom of action for its purposes. When freedom is challenged, a nation must first protect or establish it before the sea can be used.

HMS TRAFALGAR
(SSN) underway to her
patrol area

## Command at Sea

Distinguished theorists of maritime strategy, such as Vice Admiral Sir Philip Colomb (1832 -1899), Rear Admiral Alfred Thayer Mahan USN (1840 - 1914), Sir Julian Corbett (1854 - 1922 ) and Admiral Sir Herbert Richmond (1871 - 1946), have described the freedom to use the sea for one's own purposes and to deny its use to the enemy as *command of the sea*. They saw command of the sea as the principal objective of a *maritime campaign*. Total command of the sea, in the sense that one's own *maritime forces* are unchallenged anywhere and that an enemy is unable to carry out any maritime operations, can only be achieved by destruction of the enemy's maritime forces or their elimination in other ways. Such an undertaking against a substantial and well-equipped opponent could be costly, even if it were feasible or necessary. Since Corbett, strategists have generally acknowledged that the uncommanded sea is the norm. Nevertheless during *conflict* of any level of intensity it remains essential to ensure that an opponent is not able to frustrate one's military or commercial operations in the areas of those operations. Command of the sea that is limited in time and place is called *sea control*. While earlier theorists might not have distinguished between the concepts of command of the sea and sea control, for modern doctrinal purposes command of the sea is a useful expression for absolute sea control in the context of a particular *campaign*.

A nation might claim *maritime superiority* if it maintains the ability to establish sea control at will in any area of importance. Maritime superiority differs from command of the sea as it is a capability rather than a condition.

## Sea Control

Sea Control is defined as the condition in which one has freedom of action to use the sea for one's own purposes in specified areas and for specified periods of time and, where necessary, to deny its use to the enemy. There is likely to be a requirement for sea control across the spectrum of conflict. At the lower end of the spectrum, maritime forces may be used to ensure freedom of navigation by a *deterrent* presence in areas where illegal acts or constraints are being threatened to merchant shipping. At the highest end it may be necessary to use a huge array of maritime power to eliminate an enemy's ability to challenge sea control over large areas of ocean. The need for sea control is not dependent upon the existence of a substantial threat. If there is any risk to freedom of action, sea control is necessary. If the risk is small, the capabilities that will be needed can be correspondingly modest.

Early achievement and retention of the necessary level of sea control will, almost without exception, be a component of any major maritime or expeditionary campaign or operation. However there can be no absolute guarantee of protection from attack at sea unless command of the sea has been achieved. Sea control must be related to acceptable risk. For operations to take place, a working level of sea control must be achieved to provide sufficient freedom of

HMS
NORTHUMBERLAND
(Type 23) and Merlin
MK1 helicopter

1. AP3000 Air Power Doctrine.

action within an acceptable level of risk. If sea control remains in dispute in a certain area, each side will be forced to operate in the face of considerable risk. However sea control is unlikely to be an end in itself. Rather Sea control is necessary to allow use of the sea for further purposes.

Sea control comprises *control* of the surface and sub-surface environments and of the airspace above the area of control. The control of airspace is also one of degree. The minimum requirement for a successful operation is a *favourable air situation*[1]. *Air superiority*[1] will be a requirement for sea control where a robust challenge from the air is possible. *Air supremacy*[1] is a necessary precondition of command of the sea.

The geographical extent of sea control may vary from local control around a single unit to domination of very large sea areas. In many cases, such as the protection of ports and anchorages and for amphibious operations, it must be achieved and maintained up to the shoreline. Indeed maritime forces will often need to maintain air superiority across the shoreline and some distance inshore. Because of confinement and congestion, attaining sea control of *littoral* regions is a more complex task.

Sea Harrier Fighter Attack 2 (F/A2) ready for take off from HMS ILLUSTRIOUS (CVS)

## Battlespace Dominance

*Battlespace dominance*[2] embraces control over the environments of the entire *battlespace*; the surface, subsurface, air, land and space environments, and the electromagnetic spectrum. Achievement of battlespace dominance in an area will entail sea control of the sea portions of that area. The concept of battlespace dominance is useful in *joint* and littoral operations where there is a need to maintain freedom of action ashore.

## Sea Denial

Sea Denial is exercised when one party denies another the ability to control a maritime area without either wishing or being able to control that area himself. Sea denial is not a distinct concept from sea control as denial of the enemy's freedom of action is an aspect of sea control. However the concept is only applicable when full sea control is not exercised by choice or out of necessity. At the operational and tactical levels a zone of sea denial may be used as part of the outer defence of a force or area, or as a way of *containing* enemy forces. At the strategic level sea denial can be used in a *guerre de course* or sustained attack upon a nation's shipping to prevent reinforcement and to sap national morale and the ability to wage *war*.

## Fleet in Being

A nation deprived of maritime superiority might choose, or be forced, to adopt a strategy of *fleet in being*. By avoiding confrontation with a superior enemy, a nation can preserve its own maritime forces while continuing to threaten those of the enemy. The risk of attack complicates the enemy's choice of options. The threat from a fleet in being can prevent superior opposing forces from establishing their desired levels of sea control by diverting forces to other tasks, such as *blockade or containment*, and as such is a method of sea denial. A fleet in being can *compel* the enemy to concentrate his forces in a valuable area, or around valuable units,

2. Coined by the United States Navy.

**Guerre de Course & Fleet in Being**

The strategy of the German Navy during the First World War provides examples of the use of guerre de course and fleet in being. The German High Seas Fleet largely remained in harbour during the war, tying down the bulk of the Royal Navy which had to watch the North Sea while the guerre de course offensive by the U-boats attempted to strangle trade in the Atlantic and Mediterranean. Although this strategy was ultimately unsuccessful and helped lead to mutiny in the German Fleet, the defence against it did significantly constrain the strategic flexibility of the Royal Navy.

cause him to route his passage to his disadvantage or to amend his operational plans.

## Maritime Power Projection

Sea control ensures freedom of action above, on and below the surface of the sea. The projection of maritime power is the application of maritime power from the sea to influence events on land directly. It exploits sea control to achieve *access* to the coast and deliver power ashore in the form of amphibious forces, *organic* aircraft, land attack weapons and special forces.

*Maritime power projection* is a concept that has broad application both during hostilities and for *crisis management*. In a crisis power projection capability is an important contributor to *naval diplomacy* providing the principal seaborne instruments for *coercion* and reassurance. The sailing of power projection forces demonstrates political resolve without a specific statement of commitment. They can poise at sea for long periods providing clear evidence of intent and purpose. Naval diplomacy is discussed in more detail in Chapter 5. A maritime power projection force can provide the main or the lead elements for an *intervention* operation, or a *Non-Combatant Evacuation Operation*, and provide a mobile base for humanitarian or peace support operations.

Maritime power projection forces form part of the maritime component of a national *expeditionary* capability.

During hostilities maritime power projection forces can use the sea to provide access to territory that is less accessible by land and air and to apply *manoeuvre from the sea.*

## The Significance of Land Warfare Concepts for Maritime Doctrine

*At the Operational and Strategic Levels.* At the operational and strategic levels maritime warfare acquires some of the geographic characteristics of land warfare. The geographic relationship of events at sea to those ashore will usually be important to the operational commander. The apportionment, sustainment and protection of maritime *logistics* at the operational level are of similar concern to a maritime commander as those of ground forces to a land commander. The operational commander will have the problem of consolidating his logistic shipping and, perhaps, of setting up a separate tactical operation to protect consolidation shipping and reinforcements. It would be wrong to underestimate the distinctive nature of the maritime environment, in particular its vastness, featurelessness, absence of impediments to movement, and the difficulties of achieving and avoiding encounter. However, at the operational and strategic level joint doctrinal concepts are likely to prevail. These concepts demand careful study by maritime commanders and staffs. Some of these concepts such as *centre of gravity, decisive points, tempo, simultaneity* and the *culminating point* are discussed in Chapter 6.

*At the Tactical Level.* In achieving and maintaining sea control, maritime forces operate at the tactical level in a multidimensional field (see Chapter 3). Sea control is normally a temporary condition and there is no direct parallel to the progressive advance across and control of territory. Concepts used in ground warfare such as *lines of operation, lines of support,* the *forward line of own troops,* and *deep, close*

**3.** Capital letters are used to distinguish Manoeuvre and Warfare as a style of fighting from manoeuvre as a combat function.

HMS ARK ROYAL (CVS) with RFAs OLWEN (AO) and FORT AUSTIN (AFS)

and *rear operations*, which define a land battlefield in terms of geography, function and time, have no direct analogies in warfare at sea at the tactical level. A commander of a tactical formation is likely to have *organic logistics* in the form of tankers and stores ships and may feel detached from any lines of support. In particular he is unlikely to be as constrained as a land commander by the movement of his logistic *consolidation*. This is not to imply that lines of support have no relevance at the tactical level. Indeed a tactical commander may have protection of shipping as his mission. In a joint campaign, however, and specifically during power projection operations, these concepts of land warfare become relevant. Indeed during an amphibious assault the forward line of own troops is actually afloat in the early stages.

## Manoeuvre in Maritime Warfare

Manoeuvre is a concept of particular importance having two distinct but related meanings both derived originally from land warfare concepts. Firstly it describes a style of warfare[3] and secondly it is one of the ground combat functions used as the building blocks in land operations.

## Manoeuvre as a Style of Warfare

Manoeuvre Warfare has been presented by some theorists as an alternative to *Attrition Warfare.*[4] Instead of seeking to destroy an enemy's physical substance by the cumulative effect of superior firepower (Attrition Warfare), the goal of Manoeuvre Warfare is to incapacitate an enemy: disrupting his fighting system *(systemic disruption)* by concentrating s uperior force against that element of his fighting system most likely to cause incapacitation.

Theoretically Manoeuvre Warfare offers the possibility of results disproportionately greater than the resources applied, and thus the chance of success for the weaker side. It may also be a very cost effective style for a stronger opponent, allowing him to achieve success while minimizing losses. It can also fail completely if disruption does not occur as predicted. Therefore, in its pure form, Manoeuvre Warfare would entail an element of inherent risk not present in an operational concept relying largely on overwhelming force as a means of destruction.

In reality any campaign will contain elements of both Manoeuvre and Attrition styles. The threat or actual delivery of selective but overwhelming attrition against a key vulnerability can bring about the systemic disruption sought by Manoeuvre, while a series of successful Manoeuvre actions at one *level of war* may bring about cumulative effects of destruction that wear down an enemy at a higher level.

## Manoeuvre as a Style of Warfare in the Maritime Context

Historically and from the standpoint of modern *doctrine,* a navy does not have a choice between Manoeuvre and other styles of warfare. Manoeuvre Warfare theory is the intelligent use of force and is a logical development of the Principles of War, particularly the principles of surprise, flexibility, concentration of force and economy of effort. Maritime forces have the combination of *mobility,* firepower, flexibility and responsive *Command and Control* systems that is ideal for

**4.** It may be argued that Attrition Warfare is not an accurate general term for the range of more geographically static alternatives to Manoeuvre Warfare because attrition is a necessary component of any style of combat. However, the comparison of Manoeuvre and Attrition styles has been used by many theorists and helps to explain the modern meaning of Manoeuvre Warfare.

5. Army Doctrine Publication Volume I: Operations.

Manoeuvre Warfare. It may be considered to be more an attitude of mind than an operational blueprint. The historical debate is significant, however, because it reveals some important doctrinal points:

- Success in modern warfare against a well-equipped enemy requires superior intelligence, a quicker decision-making cycle, flexible and agile forces and systems that can deliver selective firepower at great range.

- Intelligence must be involved in all operational decision making.

- Opportunities for systemic disruption at the strategic and operational levels should be sought. Systemic disruption is discussed in Chapter 6.

- Strategic and operational surprise may be difficult to achieve against an enemy with similar or superior intelligence and surveillance capabilities.

- There will always be a trade-off between risk and return. At those points at which force is to be brought to bear against an enemy, risk should be minimized by achieving an adequate superiority of force and surprise.

- The development of Manoeuvre Warfare theory has been a stimulus for interest in operational art and the operational level of war. Indeed, many of the concepts of joint operational level doctrine are drawn from Manoeuvre Warfare theory, in particular that of the centre of gravity which is discussed in Chapter 6.

## Manoeuvre from the Sea as a Combat Function

The ground combat function of manoeuvre seeks "a position of advantage with respect to the enemy from which force can be threatened or applied".[5] An important role of maritime power projection forces, particularly amphibious forces, is to provide manoeuvre from the sea in this sense. Firepower can create the conditions for successful

## Manoeuvre from the Sea

Two outstanding examples of manoeuvre from the sea in which the Royal Navy played significant parts were the landings at Inchon in 1950 during the Korean War and the employment of amphibious forces in the 1991 Gulf War. In September 1950, three months after the North Korean invasion of the South the Northern forces had driven the United Nations forces into an area about Pusan in the far south of the peninsula. US Marines covered by the gunfire of two British and two American cruisers, stormed ashore at the port of Inchon near the South Korean capital of Seoul which was soon recaptured. This surprise amphibious attack struck the Northern forces in the flank, cut their lines of communication and caused their rapid collapse and retreat. Only massive Chinese intervention saved the day for the communist cause. In the Gulf War two US Marine Corps brigades first carried out a *demonstration* landing in Oman, then *poised* at sea. The effect was to tie down several Iraqi divisions in defence of the Kuwaiti coastline. On both occasions Royal Navy warships assisted in providing escort and barrier defence. In the Gulf the Royal Navy also provided the key mine countermeasures capability.

RFA Sir GALAHAD (LSL) off loading onto a beach through her bow doors

**6.** For instance, Herbert Rosinski "Mahan and World War II: A Commentary from the United States" in The Development of Naval Thought.

**7.** Carl von Clausewitz (1780 - 1831) On War

manoeuvre by providing the protection to cover movement into a favourable position, by disrupting or deceiving an enemy so that he cannot effectively react, or by exposing vulnerabilities that can be exploited by manoeuvre. However movement and firepower do not, on their own, equate to manoeuvre. Manoeuvre is used to create favourable combat conditions. Tasks associated with maritime power projection to allow manoeuvre from the sea are discussed in Chapter 5.

## Proactive and Reactive Choices in Strategic Operational Planning

A maritime power projection operation is by definition a *proactive* operation in that it involves seizing the initiative by forward operations in which forces are moved to invite contact with the enemy. This is not to say that it is necessarily offensive. For instance, the mission may be to effect withdrawal or evacuation. In contrast the task of achieving sea control will present the commander with both proactive operational and reactive options in which the initiative is retained by drawing the enemy into contact.

It is important to distinguish clearly between the offense and the initiative. Some have argued that the offensive is the stronger form of warfare at sea[6] in contrast to Clausewitz's[7] maxim, derived from land combat on a linear battlefield, that the defence is the stronger form of waging war. The line of argument is that in a non-linear maritime environment the naval commander frequently has no clearly defined perimeter along which to marshal defensive forces, and may expect air, surface or underwater attack from any direction. It may therefore take large resources to construct a robust defence while a single offensive unit, for example a submarine operating in waters close to an enemy shore, can generate disproportionate defensive effort.

However, a slavish adherence to "the offensive" can lead to important strategic and operational errors, such as the British failure to convoy in favour of "hunting groups" during the First World War. A more useful analysis of modern maritime combat is the division into proactive and reactive elements. To be successful in maritime combat a commander must seize and maintain the initiative to force a response to his actions, thereby ensuring that engagements take place on his own terms. In doing so the commander should exploit, where possible, the advantages both of reactive posture (for instance concentration of forces around the shipping at risk to draw the enemy to destruction) or proactive operations (such as *distraction* of enemy forces).

A classical proactive method of achieving sea control, frequently advocated and used by the Royal Navy in the past and referred to earlier in this chapter, is to seek out the enemy to bring him to decisive battle thereby destroying his forces and eliminating his capability to challenge sea control. Other maritime operations can then proceed unthreatened. Historically this course was not simply a matter of *élan* but reflected Britain's qualitative superiority over its enemies. To be effective it will generally require a large *balance of advantage* in maritime forces. The enemy may also have the option of declining battle and operating a fleet in being.

Other proactive methods can be considered under the concept of military containment, which constitutes constraining an enemy's forces in areas clear of those in which sea control is required. Containment can be achieved by *close* or *distant blockade* (See Chapter 5) or by *distracting* an enemy's maritime forces by posing an overriding threat to his critical interests.

Reactive methods of achieving sea control comprise the direct *screening* of formations and convoys, and the use of defensive barriers of sub-surface, surface and air forces.

Because of the huge size of the maritime arena, the variety of air, surface and sub-surface threats, and vagaries in detection and prosecution of targets, no single system or layer of protection is likely to be adequate. For this reason sea control is usually effected by a combination of proactive

Seaking MK6 (ASW)
helicopter about to go
into the dip

and reactive methods. Probabilities of effectiveness of the various methods are thus aggregated to provide adequate levels of protection. This principle of defence in depth is demonstrated most clearly in the *layered defence* of a formation of high value or an *amphibious objective area (AOA)* and is illustrated in Chapter 9.

Methods of achieving sea control are discussed in more detail under "Maritime Power at Sea" in Chapter 5.

## Summary - NATO's Principles of Maritime Operations

This chapter has been devoted to concepts of the military or combat governed use of maritime force. Many of these concepts have application during sustained hostilities (war). However the concepts of sea control and power projection in their modern interpretation have relevance throughout the spectrum of conflict. While the *Principles of War (Annex A)* govern military operations in all environments, the Major NATO Commanders have defined four principles of maritime operations. They bring together the themes of this chapter, and capture the essence of Manoeuvre Warfare and the proactive/reactive dilemma. The three that are particularly relevant to combat operations are: Seizing the Initiative; Containment; and Defence in Depth. The fourth is *Presence* which is discussed in the next chapter (Chapter 5).

### NATO's Principles of Maritime Operations

Seizing the Initiative

Containment

Defence in Depth

Presence

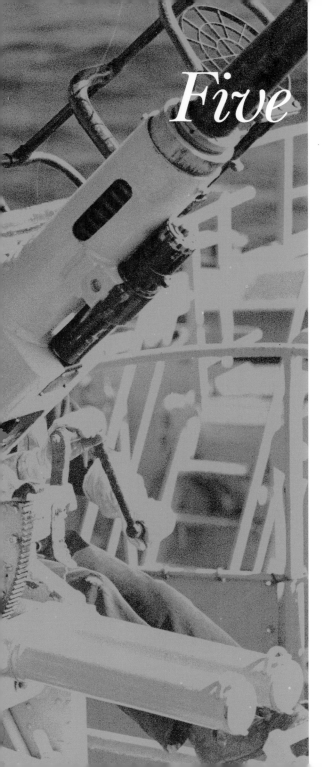

# Five

# 5

# The Application of Maritime Power

This chapter reviews the range of tasks that *maritime forces*, might be called upon to undertake either on their own, or more probably as part of *joint* or *combined* forces. Using the distinctions drawn in Chapter 2, maritime power can be sub-divided into *military* or combat governed, *constabulary* and benign applications.

1. Initial capital letters
are used for the United
Kingdom's Military Tasks,
as defined in the annual
Statement on the
Defence Estimates (see
Chapter 1) throughout
this publication to
distinguish them from
the maritime tasks
discussed in this chapter,
and other tasks

# The Military Application of Maritime Power

The applications of maritime power discussed in this section are governed by the concepts of *sea control* and *power projection* explained in Chapter 4. This is not to say that *violence* or *combat* will be a necessary feature of these tasks, but it is the potential of the forces for combat that underpins their effectiveness in any military application. Even when maintaining *presence* in peacetime or when engaged in symbolic acts of *naval diplomacy*, it is the combat capability of the formation or unit, and the evidence that it provides of force that might follow, which carry the diplomatic message of national interest, will and intent.

Military applications of maritime power do not fall neatly into the two categories of power projection and sea control, because a degree of sea control is an enabling requirement for most tasks[1] in *conflict*. However a useful distinction can be made between applications of power from the sea which are broadly power projection tasks, and those at sea of which sea control is the essence.

HMS TRENCHANT (SSN) leaving harbour

# Martime Power from the Sea

**2.** Military Tasks 1.1 & 2.1

## Nuclear Deterrence

The maintenance of a secure *strategic nuclear deterrent* is the first Military Task[2] of the Royal Navy. The United Kingdom's instruments of strategic nuclear deterrence are deployed at sea because the stealth of nuclear powered submarines makes them extremely hard to find and destroy. They are not therefore liable to preemptive attack or counter-attack. Nuclear weapons have great *reach* and variable direction of attack when deployed in nuclear powered submarines. Although a nuclear ballistic missile submarine is highly survivable when on patrol, it may require support from sea control forces during deployment. Trident submarines have the flexibility to contribute to the *sub-strategic* component of our deterrence forces, and in due course will provide this capability in its entirety. A sub-strategic nuclear deterrent provides the capability to deliver more limited nuclear attacks than that maintained for strategic nuclear deterrence and is a flexible and essential element of our nuclear deterrent posture.

## Combat Operations Against the Land

Maritime combat power can be projected ashore using *manoeuvre from the sea* through organic attack aircraft, submarine and surface launched land attack missiles, *naval gunfire support (NGS)*, amphibious forces and special forces. Amphibious operations can be *assaults, raids, demonstrations, feints* or *withdrawals*. Operations ashore will usually be joint, requiring effective co-operation and a clearly understood command structure. Contribution to a ground *campaign* by specific *manoeuvre* operations from seaward can be used for *envelopment, turning movements* or *infiltration* and *interdiction* of key vulnerabilities ashore. *Poising* afloat, power projection forces can provide *distraction* by tying down a disproportionate number of enemy forces in defending a coastline, rendering them unavailable for other operations. The effect can be enhanced by raids, feints or

HMS FEARLESS (LPD)
off loading

demonstrations. Distraction is an important aspect of maritime leverage which is discussed in Chapter 3.

Combat operations against the land include the following tasks:

***Advance Force Operations.*** To prepare an *amphibious objective area (AOA)*. They may include the insertion of personnel by submarine or aircraft (see Chapter 9), precursor mine countermeasures operations, and bombardment by naval gunfire support (NGS) forces and aircraft.

***Amphibious Assault.*** Specialist amphibious troops can be landed to secure a *lodgement area* by seizing a *beachhead* or other means of entry such as ports or airfields. This lodgement area can then be used as a springboard for further operations, either by the landing force, or by follow on forces inserted through the lodgement area. They can be

used as part of a campaign plan to provide leverage, to

contribute to *simultaneity* and to increase the *tempo* of an operation. Ideally amphibious assault requires: the establishment of robust sea control[3] around the assault forces and over the area of sea adjacent to the assault, but at minimum a *favourable air situation*, which must also extend over the landward portion of the amphibious objective area; creation of a beachhead to allow heavier forces and *materiel* to land; and the provision of air support for forces ashore. Amphibious assault may be used to seize advanced logistic facilities such as a sheltered anchorage, port or airhead for maritime forces.

*Amphibious Raid.* Amphibious forces may be landed for a discrete task, on completion of which a withdrawal takes place. The period over which sea control must be maintained may be shorter for a raid than for an assault. Raids may be ends in themselves, or may be used to distract, or to provide simultaneity. While they are often carried out by comparatively small forces, they can be up to Brigade strength.

*Amphibious Feints and Demonstrations.* While assaults and raids involve the landing of troops, amphibious forces can also be used without landing. They can deceive an enemy (a feint) or demonstrate capability (a demonstration) with the effect of: tying down forces; creating uncertainty; or, as a *coercive* act of naval diplomacy (see below), to reinforce a diplomatic message.

*Amphibious Withdrawal.* A withdrawal is a normal operation for amphibious forces as the value of leverage is lost if they are committed for extended periods ashore on non-specialist tasks. Sea based forces can also secure an exit route for land forces, both for tactical and unplanned withdrawals and can provide for mass evacuation.

*Naval Support to Land Operations.* Organic naval aircraft can contribute to *strategic air offensive, counter-air, anti-surface force (land and sea)*, and *combat support air operations*, all of which

3. Which may include air superiority.

may be supporting land or joint campaign objectives. Submarines and, indeed, surface ships armed with *land attack missiles* could contribute to an attack on important shore targets. Naval gunfire support can provide fire support to ground forces. Maritime electronic capabilities can contribute significant intelligence support and naval surface to air missiles provide air defence over coastal areas.

***Land Attack in Support of Sea Control.*** Power projection forces (including special forces) may be employed as part of a sea control campaign to destroy enemy maritime forces in harbours, ports and air bases, and enabling capabilities such as *command and control* systems and logistics. Alternatively, they can be used to secure a land flank for sea control forces.

## Combat Operations in Defence of Forces Ashore
Maritime forces can assist in the protection of land forces or territory by providing a sea based defensive barrier. Broadly they could defend the maritime flank against manoeuvre from the sea. More specifically they could contribute to air defence, supplementing land based forces or, in the early stages of establishing a lodgement area, supply total air defence capability. Within this is the potential of sea based forces to provide defence against Theatre Ballistic Missiles.

## Evacuation Operations
Maritime forces would usually contribute to *Non-Combatant Evacuation Operations (NEO)* as part of a joint or combined force. However, where airfields and commercial ports are not available, an independent naval operation across a beachhead may be necessary. *Naval forces* may also be used to poise in theatre as a precaution should an evacuation become necessary as a result of local instability. The host nation may be able to provide for the security of the evacuation in which case the United Kingdom or coalition forces would provide assistance to the process and perhaps *lift*. This type of evacuation is referred to as a *Services Assisted*

## Evacuation Operations

The use of maritime forces in evacuation operations was demonstrated during the civil war between government and rival factions at Aden in January 1986. The Royal Yacht, later supported by HM Ships NEWCASTLE, JUPITER and RFA BRAMBLELEAF, evacuated 1379 men, women and children of 55 different nationalities from the besieged town. The majority were evacuated by the Royal Yacht's own boats over an open beach.

*Evacuation.* Alternatively forces may be required for the protection of the evacuees as well as to provide an avenue of evacuation and transport - an operation known as a *Services Protected Evacuation.* In extreme cases an evacuation may amount to an amphibious raid. Amphibious forces will land, secure and defend beachheads and airheads, establish mustering points for evacuees and the routes linking them, move the evacuees to safety, and finally withdraw. Amphibious forces are well suited to a Services Protected Evacuation in that they are self-sustaining, require little or no in-country or host nation support, and have the capability to respond rapidly to any deterioration in the situation. The decision to evacuate nationals is the responsibility of the local British Ambassador or other Head of Mission whose staff will normally give instructions to evacuees. Command and control arrangements must integrate the Mission and any Special Forces contribution. National and NATO *Joint Theatre Plans* include contingency plans for evacuation.

## Naval Force in Support of Diplomacy

Naval diplomacy is the use of naval forces as a diplomatic instrument in support of foreign policy. In the joint context in which maritime forces will frequently operate, it is sometimes known as *armed suasion,* a concept to which ground and air forces make their own distinctive contribution. Naval diplomacy is action designed to influence the

**4.** Sir James Cable
Gunboat Diplomacy
1919 - 1991
(Third Edition)

leadership of a state or group of states in peacetime and all situations short of full *hostilities*. Naval diplomacy can be used on the one hand to support or reassure and can be a significant contributor to *coalition building*. On the other hand it can be used to deter and coerce trouble-makers. Naval forces have particular uses in that they can poise in theatre at an early stage in a potential crisis with minimal diplomatic preparation. They offer a versatile and graduated response to a developing *crisis*. By exploiting the freedom of the seas naval forces can often be the first units involved in a crisis area and once present can poise for an extended period. If required they can quickly and easily withdraw, without a public and possibly embarrassing retreat or abandonment of territory. They can maintain presence without occupation; coercion without *embroilment*.

Sir James Cable[4], himself a distinguished diplomat and maritime strategist, called naval diplomacy "Gunboat Diplomacy" and defined it as:

"..... the use or threat of limited naval force, otherwise than as an act of war, in order to secure advantage or to avert loss, either in the furtherance of an international dispute or else against foreign nationals within the territory or the jurisdiction of their own state."

For the purposes of *doctrine* naval diplomacy can be broadly categorised as follows:

*Presence.* When naval diplomacy is exercised in a general way involving deployments, port visits, exercising and routine operating in areas of interest, it is known as presence. A traditional way in which naval forces demonstrate *presence* is by visiting foreign ports to remind the local inhabitants of the effectiveness of the navy and the state that owns it. There is no threat of force; instead the vessel and her ships company act as ambassadors, whose function is to make a favourable impression on the local population. Warships are unique in their international acceptability and ability to make this kind of impact. The presence of a naval vessel in an area may be the primary symbol of national commitment, for example HMS ENDURANCE in Antarctica. Presence is both a national and an Alliance task; indeed, the contribution of presence to stability and deterrence is considered by the Major NATO Commanders to be so important that it has been adopted by NATO as a principle governing the use of maritime forces (See Chapter 4). The term *forward presence* is used to express a strategic decision to deploy forces for presence into or close to theatres of interest or concern.

***Symbolic Use.*** Naval forces can be used purely to signal a message to a specific government while not in themselves posing any threat to an opponent or providing significant military assistance to a friend.

### Symbolic Use of Naval Force

"In order to clothe the arrival of our new Ambassador, Lord Halifax, in the United States with every circumstance of importance, I arranged that our newest and strongest battleship, the KING GEORGE V, with a proper escort of destroyers, should carry him and his wife across the ocean." Sir Winston Churchill on a decision made in 1941 before the United States had entered the Second World War (W S Churchill The Grand Alliance London: Cassell 1950). [Reproduced with permission of Curtis Brown Ltd, London on behalf of the Estate of Sir Winston S Churchill. Copyright the Estate of Sir Winston S Churchill.]

***Coercion.*** When a stronger message is required, naval diplomacy can take the form of the employment of carefully tailored forces with an offensive capability. This can act as a signal of will and greater force to follow, or encouragement of a friend or ally by providing some reinforcement. The threat or use of limited offensive action is coercion which may be designed to deter a possible aggressor or to *compel* him to comply with a diplomatic *demarche* or resolution.

*Preventive, Precautionary and Preemptive Naval Diplomacy.*
There may be occasions when the Government or Alliance
wishes to be in a position to influence events, particularly in
the early stages of a crisis, but specific policy objectives may
be unclear beyond the need to declare interest and avoid
*maldeployment.* In these situations tailored naval forces operating under carefully crafted rules of engagement can poise
in theatre for subsequent use when national or Allied objectives have been refined. In the language of peace support
operations (see below) naval forces may be significant
contributors to *preventive deployments* for *crisis prevention.*

### Maritime Operations in the Spanish Civil War

Modern maritime operations in support of diplomacy and
humanitarian objectives are not new, but a return to more normal
activities after the aberration of the cold war with its emphasis on
preparation in "peacetime" for the highest levels of conflict. Good
examples of the previous "normal" patterns from earlier this century
were the activities of the Royal Navy in the Spanish Civil War (1936 -
1939). British warships were used to prevent interference with
shipping by Spanish warships not granted belligerent rights by the
international community, to break illegal blockades, to prevent Italian
submarines from covertly sinking ships bound for Spain, to evacuate
personnel threatened by one side or the other and to symbolize by
their presence on patrol the principle of non-intervention.

## Peace Support Operations

Maritime forces can contribute a variety of tasks in peace
support operations (see Box). Many of these are discussed
in detail elsewhere in this chapter. From a doctrinal viewpoint it is the diplomatic environment and complicated
command and control arrangements that characterize
peace support by maritime forces. These operations will be
carried out under the authority of United Nations or the
OSCE (see Chapter 1) but NATO, the WEU, European Union and other regional organizations may also be involved.

United Kingdom forces may be operating under the command of the United Nations, under national command in co-ordination with UN forces or under NATO or other coalition command. The hierarchy of military activity (see Figure 2.1) will not be clearly defined during peace support operations. The presence of civilian UN authorities, civilian staff of non-governmental organizations such as the Red Cross, the multiplicity of national and international operational and tactical headquarters in theatre and the intricate and frequently ad hoc co-ordination arrangements between them will all serve to complicate the situation.

### Yugoslavia - Maritime Peace Support Operations

The Royal Navy's contribution to UNPROFOR in the former Yugoslavia has included:

- fighter aircraft patrols (supported by shore based AWACS aircraft and air to air refuelling) in support of the No Fly Zone from a carrier in the Adriatic.

- reconnaissance and *close air support* to troops ashore.

- support helicopters based ashore for casualty evacuation.

- combat service support to the British UNPROFOR contingent.

- embargo operations.

The carrier's ability to position herself close to the operational area and minimise the effects of adverse weather makes her organic aircraft ideal for short notice tasking. RN destroyers and frigates, acting under NATO and WEU command have enforced the UN embargoes, and in the first two and a half years NATO and WEU vessels boarded over 3,345 ships and diverted more than 653 suspected violators. Heavy equipment has been moved to the theatre by sea and a *Royal Fleet Auxiliary ship* alongside in Split has provided accommodation and stores support. On two occasions RN ships have been used as neutral territory to host meetings between warring factions, in one case this resulted in the lifting of the seige of Dubrovnik.

**5.** AJP1(A). Allied Joint Operations Doctrine.

**6.** Army Field Manual Wider Peacekeeping.

**7.** Cantonment is a demobilization activity that is included under wider peacekeeping. RN and RM personnel supervised the contonment of vessels under UNTAC in Cambodia from 1992 to 1993.

**8.** Army Doctrine Publication Volume I: Operations. The expression "Peacemaking" is often frequently confused with "peace enforcement" but actually means diplomatic activity to restore peace after a conflict has begun.

**9.** Included in wider peacekeeping as denial of movement.

The categories of peace support activity[5] are:

**Conflict Prevention** which is principally a diplomatic function. Naval diplomacy may have a part to play in providing presence and *preventive deployment.*

**Peacekeeping.** The insertion of observer missions and interposition of forces are the two forms of traditional *peacekeeping.* The maritime contribution to traditional peacekeeping is a constabulary task and is therefore discussed under the sub-title "Constabulary Tasks". However in the environment of Wider Peacekeeping (see below) peacekeeping forces may need to be prepared for military applications of force.

**Wider Peacekeeping.**[6] This expression is frequently used to describe peace support operations that are conducted with the consent of belligerents but in an environment that may be highly volatile. However observer missions and interposition are categorized as *peacekeeping.* Wider peacekeeping therefore includes conflict *prevention, demobilization operations, cantonment*[7] of vessels, military assistance (in the context of peace support), humanitarian relief and the guarantee and denial of movement. It excludes *peace enforcement.* Wider peacekeeping consists of a mixture of constabulary, benign and military applications of military power.

**Peace Enforcement.** Operations carried out to restore peace between belligerent parties who do not all consent to *intervention* and who may be engaged in combat are *peace enforcement operations.*[8] These are *military* operations and are quite distinct in character from peacekeeping. Forces engaged in or supporting peace enforcement may need to initiate combat and carry out coercive acts against one or more parties. For this they will require a mandate to use military force and appropriate rules of engagement. A naval force poised off a disputed area may apply coercion to persuade or dissuade belligerents. Maritime forces can be used: for air defence and the maintenance of *no fly zones*[9]; to provide mine clearance for *access* to the coast; to evacuate nationals and casualties; to facilitate a withdrawal of ground forces; to provide helicopter mobility in theatre and an afloat logistic base; to enforce sanctions, an *embargo* or, a full *blockade*; and to provide amphibious support to ground combat operations.

***Peace Building.*** These tasks are essentially benign and are discussed under the sub-title "Benign Tasks".

## Peace Support Operations - Maritime Tasks

- Active monitoring of a sea area for infringement of sanctions/embargo

- Patrolling and monitoring a maritime cease fire line or demilitarized zone

- Enforcement of sanctions/embargo

- Supervising cantonment of vessels

- Contribution of *organic* aircraft to enforcement of a *no fly zone* and *combat air support*

- Contribution of organic helicopters for in theatre movement of peacekeeping forces and humanitarian aid, and casualty evacuation

- Contribution of amphibious forces to ground peace support operations

- Maintenance of an amphibious capability in theatre to permit withdrawal of peacekeeping forces, aid workers and other civilians

- Provision of seaborne medical and other logistic and humanitarian resources where access by land is difficult

- Assistance to seaborne refugees

- Provision of a neutral platform for peace negotiations

- Mine countermeasures to provide access or contribute to a new peace

# Maritime Power at Sea
## Operations against Enemy Forces

*Interdiction of Enemy Maritime Forces, Sealift and Commercial Shipping.* Denying the enemy the ability to use maritime forces and *sealift* to move resources and conduct trade, erodes his strategic capability to wage *war*. At the operational level interdiction hampers an enemy's attempts at reinforcement or manoeuvre from the sea and frustrates his sea control and sea denial operations. Interdiction operations can be conducted against shipping and aircraft at sea, in harbour, in the air or on land.

*Blockade.*[10] Blockade is a combat operation to prevent access to, or departure from, a defined area of an enemy's coast and waters. It can be used operationally as a method of achieving sea control or sea denial through containment. Strategically it may also be used as an extreme form of sanctions enforcement. During full hostilities, it can prevent reinforcement, resupply, and maritime trade, and thus deprive an enemy of the national material and moral resources necessary to continue hostilities. To be recognized under International Law, a blockade must: have been declared and notified to all concerned; be effective; and, be applied impartially to ships of all nations. A blockading force has the legal right to seize in prize any merchant ship, be it enemy or neutral, which attempts to run the blockade either inwards or outwards. The blockade can be either close, denying an enemy access to or from his ports, or distant, denying the access to a sea area through which all ships must pass in order to reach the enemy's territory.

*Containment by Distraction.* Containment can also be achieved by posing a threat to an enemy's critical interests so that he must retain maritime forces in defence of those interests. The threat to these enemy interests may take the form of a direct challenge to the enemy's own sea control forces or power projection forces that could threaten targets ashore. Containment of the Soviet Navy in this manner,

**10.** Blockade is often used loosely and incorrectly to mean "embargo or sanctions enforcement".

**Left:** Single Role Mine Hunter (SRMH)

95

HMS CORNWALL
(Type 22)

in order to maintain freedom of action in the Atlantic and Pacific, was an important component of the United States' Navy's Forward Maritime Strategy of the 1980s.

***Area Sea Control Operations.*** These operations are essentially static and are conducted using long range surveillance systems and weapon delivery systems over large areas of sea. Their targets are principally enemy aircraft, ships and submarines which are in transit into attack positions. Careful co-ordination of command and control is required to allow a mobile force under afloat command to pass through areas of Area Operations under the control of commanders ashore without mutual interference or *fratricide*.

***Establishment and Maintenance of Exclusion Zones.*** Although exclusion zones have no accepted status under international law, *Military* and *Total Exclusion Zones* serve both a military and diplomatic function. In conflict they offer a means of simplifying a sea control problem through the promulgation of an intention to maintain *sea denial* over a specific area. Their enforcement requires rules of engagement that allow the selective use of combat. Diplomatically they are a way of enhancing coercive action by declaring resolve to use combat if necessary.

***Barrier Operations.*** Barriers of sea control forces can be set up where geographic or oceanographic features or operational constraints will channel or concentrate attacking enemy forces.

***Defended Areas.*** In the past, attempts to defend sea lanes directly have always failed because the available sensors and weapons were not able to prevent attacking forces from penetrating the defences. There are some defined areas of water, however, which may require to be cleared of hostile forces by *precursor operations* (see below) and subsequently protected against incursion. These might include straits, geographical approaches, convoy assembly and dispersal areas, and an *AOA*. With modern capabilities for long range surveillance, maritime forces may now be tasked to provide area sea control and static *layered defence* of these areas, though the difficulty of achieving area sea control should not be underestimated..

***Precursor (Advance Sea Control) Operations.*** These are operations in advance of a main force, particularly a power projection force, to eliminate enemy sea denial forces such as conventional submarines and mines. Advance operations in littoral areas may take a considerable time to reduce the risk to acceptable levels, which may compromise surprise. However, by the same token, they can contribute to the credibility of a *feint* or other *distractive* device.

***Layered Defence (Close and Distant Screening).*** Moving layers of air, anti-submarine and anti-surface defence are organized about a unit, formation of high value or perhaps even a sea area of importance in screens and patrol areas. Specific units or formations within the screens are allocated sectors or zones of responsibility. Sectors or zones ensure economy of effort and prevent mutual interference.

### Protection of Maritime Trade

The importance of maritime trade to the United Kingdom, NATO and the European Union was discussed in Chapter 3. In peacetime, naval forces maintain freedom of the seas for maritime trade by general presence and, on occasion, by *freedom of navigation operations* (see box).

*Naval Control of Shipping (NCS)*. When there is a significant risk to maritime trade, the Government may offer specific protection to merchant ships through control of merchant shipping. This protection and control would be confined to voluntary participation by ships or ships' owners and operators within a clearly defined geographical region or regions under *Regional Naval Control of Shipping* (RNCS). Mobile NCS teams for RNCS provide a flexible response to any crisis affecting allied merchant shipping, as do a range of other NCS measures, through the issue of navigational warnings, to selected advisory briefing, to accompanying, to *escorting*, and finally, to the formation of convoys for merchant ships. These are explained in more detail below. Under certain situations United Kingdom forces may be called upon to protect ships of many nationalities carrying cargoes of interest to the UK and its allies.

HMS MANCHESTER (TYPE 42) together with British merchant ship BRITISH RESOLUTION

## Freedom of Navigation Operations

If a state's claim to territorial seas is not accepted or it attempts to restrict the use of the high seas or international straits, it may be necessary to use naval forces to demonstrate intent to use those waters. It may also be necessary to prevent a state from claiming customary rights in the future. Freedom of navigation operations are designed to persuade or dissuade a government and are therefore a form of naval diplomacy. They may be symbolic or coercive. In autumn 1963 the carrier HMS VICTORIOUS and supporting forces demonstrated the right and resolve to use the Sunda Strait between Java and Sumatra by conducting an overt transit during the campaign associated with Indonesian confrontation of Malaysia.

*Methods of Protection.* Protection of maritime trade can take different forms depending upon whether the aim is to deter attacks, or to defend against them.

*Sea Control Methods.* If the threat to shipping is sufficiently great, protection will require sea control methods discussed earlier in this section. Merchant shipping may benefit from a wider sea control campaign that will offer protection in the waters through which it will pass, or a specific sea control operation may be devoted to the shipping under threat using *convoying*. Both concepts can be used within a wider sea control campaign if resources permit.

*Convoying.* When there is a severe risk to maritime trade, convoying is a tested method of reducing the scale of the sea control problem. If shipping is gathered into convoys, the area and time over which sea control must be exercised for their protection is reduced to a minimum. Convoying complicates the attacker's task and concentrates escorting forces to enhance the effectiveness of protection. However convoying is disruptive to trade. The strategic or operational decision to convoy requires a careful weighing of the balance of advantage and the opportunities for drawing the enemy into decisive action.

**Convoy**

Naval officers have sometimes been ambivalent towards convoy. Superficially, grouping ships together seems to make them more rather than less vulnerable; "too many eggs in one basket". In fact the lessons of history are clearer on this issue than on most others. Independent shipping is always at much greater risk than convoyed shipping as it is easier to find and destroy. Before the First World War it was thought that technological development had made convoy obsolete. In the event, only the belated introduction of convoy in 1917 saved Britain from the U-boats. In the Second World War German submarine commanders only achieved their "happy times" against independent shipping. When an ocean convoy system was fully introduced in 1941, the overall level of individual U-boat kills declined, never to recover. As in the previous war, convoys could be routed round U boats located by special intelligence. When the Germans, in greater strength, turned on the convoys as their only alternative in 1942-3 they were only able to achieve successes at insupportable cost. Larger convoys proved less vulnerable than smaller, and released escorts to create groups to support convoys that intelligence revealed to be under threat. Concentrating forces around convoys at risk defeated the U boats in 1943, and for the rest of the war the ocean convoy system remained a wall against which the Germans smashed themselves with little effect.

***Distant and Close Escort.*** If there is regional tension or where there is a threat of *piracy* or attack by irregular forces, maritime forces can be on hand in theatre demonstrating presence to deter attack. When the threat is greater, distant or close escort provides more specific protection. Maritime forces can provide surveillance against threats, be positioned in the vicinity of concentrations of merchant shipping (distant escort), or remain in direct proximity to selected ships (close escort). While conducting both close and distant escort, naval forces offer a measure of defence but the concept is to deter attack through the threat of reprisals. It will rarely be possible to escort and, therefore, to defend every vessel in which case measures can be taken to enhance the defensive capability of individual merchant ships.

## Constabulary (Policing) Application of Maritime Power

*Embargo, Economic Sanctions and Quarantine Enforcement.* These tasks are frequently carried out under international mandate. As with other constabulary tasks the level of force that may be used in enforcement must be mandated to ensure legality. Forces involved may be subject to counter-attack, so a level of local sea control may be required to ensure the protection of enforcement forces. *Quarantine* is

Embargo operations - fast roping from a Lynx helicopter

normally used to restrict the egress of certain categories of cargo. These tasks are distinct from blockade which is a military application constituting an act of war and which must fulfil the requirements of international law described earlier.

*Peacekeeping.* This expression strictly means the use of observer missions and interposition forces.[11] They are carried out with the consent of the belligerent parties, in support of efforts to achieve or maintain peace. Peacekeeping forces operate with impartiality. Maritime forces have a part to play in peacekeeping. A maritime interposition force can supervise a marine or riverine demarcation line, monitor a cease fire afloat and patrol a buffer zone at sea. Alternatively, naval personnel and Royal Marine units and formations can be used as ground peacekeeping forces.

*Anti-Piracy Operations.* Operations to uphold international law to curb minor instances of piracy may be constabulary. Within territorial seas they are a national responsibility. Where piracy is rife and pirates are equipped with modern weapons and craft, the task has the same characteristics and requirements as other forms of protection of shipping including, perhaps, the need for robust sea control measures.

*Military Assistance to the Civil Power and Civil Ministries.* In the United Kingdom's *Maritime Domain* (that series of jurisdictional zones that surround the coast and those of the Dependent Territories) maritime forces perform a number of tasks on behalf of the relevant Civil Authorities known as *Miliary Aid to the Civil Power and Civil Ministries (MACP and MACM).* These consist of law enforcement and the maintenance of good order around the coast. Examples are fishery protection, assistance to HM Customs and Excise (especially drug interdiction), oil and gas field patrols, maritime counter-terrorism (MCT) and the naval patrols against arms smuggling that have been running for many years off the coast of Northern Ireland.

# Benign Application of Maritime Power

*Humanitarian and Disaster Relief.* As part of our overall security policy, Britain's armed forces have a history of contributing to regional stability by participating in humanitarian and disaster relief operations around the world. The flexibility of maritime forces and their independent logistic support makes them particularly effective in disaster relief operations following hurricanes and tropical cyclones. Under Defence Role 1 the armed forces may be required to provide disaster relief to the Dependent Territories (See MACC below) several of which are in the Caribbean where there is frequent hurricane damage. Maritime forces can also provide a comprehensive logistics base offshore for humanitarian operations in support of peace initiatives, and shipborne helicopters can provide a versatile means of transport.

### Disaster Relief

In May 1991 Bangladesh was hit by a cyclone, causing extensive flooding along coastal areas. RFA FORT GRANGE with 2 assault helicopters, 6 rigid raiding craft and some additional Royal Naval and Royal Marine personnel was deployed to assist in the delivery of much needed food and stores. She acted as an enabling asset for the local authorities in their efforts to recover from the effects of the cyclone.

*Peace Building Operations.* Naval logistic resources can be deployed for peace building from afloat bases. Another maritime contribution to peace building is the clearance of mines and other ordnance from waterways and beaches.

*Search and Rescue.* All vessels on the *high seas* are required under international law to assist in search and rescue. Nearer to home Naval aircraft, together with the Royal Air Force and civilian rescue organizations, provide continuous Search and Rescue cover around our coasts.

103

***Military Assistance to the Civil Community.*** In the United Kingdom's Maritime Domain, disaster relief and search and rescue form part of *Military Assistance to the Civil Community* (MACC) as do salvage, ordnance disposal, pollution control, hydrographic surveying and the provision of vessel traffic services in Dockyard Ports under the auspices of Queen's Harbour Masters.

***Military Assistance to Foreign and Commonwealth Governments.*** The UK government offers assistance to many foreign and Commonwealth governments, in the form of training and military education in Naval establishments, in country advisory and training teams and liaison staff. Exercising and training with the forces of other countries is of mutual benefit by increasing interoperability. Such activity can also provide a particular service to developing navies in the refinement and practice of procedures. Many navies use UK operational sea training facilities and take part in our national exercises.

# APPLICATION OF MARITIME POWER

| MILITARY | | CONSTABULARY | BENIGN |
|---|---|---|---|
| **From the Sea** *Power Projection* | **At Sea** *Sea Control* | | |
| Nuclear Deterrence • Combat Operations against the Land • Combat Operations in Defence of Land Forces • Evacuation Operations • Naval Force in Support of Diplomacy • Peace Support Operations | Operations Against Enemy Forces • Protection of Maritime Trade | Embargo, Sanctions & Quarantine Enforcement • Peacekeeping • Anti-piracy Operations • Fishery Protection • Drug Interdiction • Contraband Operations • Oil and Gas Field Patrols • Maritime Counter-Terrorism • Support to Counter-Insurgency Operations • Enforcement of Maritime Agreements | Disaster relief • Assistance to Refugees • Peace Building Operations • Search and Rescue • Salvage • Ordnance Disposal • Pollution Control • Hydrographic Surveying • Vessel Traffic Services • Military Assistance to Foreign & Commonwealth Governments |

Figure 5.1

*Six* 6

# Planning and Conducting a Campaign or Operation

*Doctrine* provides a framework of concepts for the application of military power in the context of national and multinational *joint* operations. This chapter covers the doctrinal concepts that influence the way in which a *campaign* or operation is planned and conducted.

1. See AJP1(A) *Allied Joint Operations Doctrine Chapter 4.*

2. The *Joint Commander* is an *operational commander* in his capacity as recipient and implementer of a *military strategic directive.* In the UK command system he also has some *military strategic level* functions. For a NATO campaign the *grand strategic level* is that of the North Atlantic Council and Defence Planning Committee supported by the International Staff. The military strategic level is the Military Committee supported by the International Military Staff. The Major NATO Commanders are the top tier of the *operational level.* A UK *Joint Force Commander* or *Allied Combined Joint Task Force Commander* may operate at the operational or *tactical level* depending on the scale and strategic significance of his mission.

# Introduction

The emphasis in this chapter is clearly on the operational level of military planning. As such it provides a bridge to operational and tactical level doctrinal publications, in particular *The Fighting Instructions.*

This document is not intended to provide detailed guidance on operational planning, nor to describe planning tools such as *The Commander's Estimate of the Situation* [1] (or *Commander's Appreciation*), but to provide a logical train that will set the concepts discussed in earlier chapters in a practical context. In this process the Principles of War (Annex A) provide general guidance to a commander. An accepted umbrella term for the concepts which follow is *operational art (also defined in the box on page 42).*

## Significant Concepts of Operational Art

*The Military Strategic Aim.* The policy objectives of military action will be decided at the *grand strategic level* by the Cabinet. In the context of major *war* these are often known as the nations's *war aims.* The strategic *mission* for a particular campaign in a particular theatre will be formed at the *military strategic level* in the Ministry of Defence and passed to the *operational commander* usually in the form of a *directive* from the Chief of the Defence Staff. In the UK command system, the recipient and implementer of the military strategic directive is the *Joint Commander* [2] who is supported by a Maritime Deputy.

The Joint Commander will in turn issue his own directive (agreed by the Ministry of Defence) to the *Joint Force Commander* who will normally be supported by a *Maritime Component Commander.* These in-theatre commanders may operate at the *operational or tactical levels* depending on the scale and significance of their operations. (See Figure 7.1). The maritime, ground and air components of a campaign or operation must be integrated fully to execute a single joint *concept of operations* to fulfil the military strategic aim.

A mission may not in itself be identical to a strategic aim.

Sea Harriers from
HMS ARK ROYAL
refuelling from a
RAF VC10 tanker

A mission statement may be fairly broad and brief and may spawn a number of objectives. The operational commander may need to sort these objectives into a principal *aim* and a number of subordinate objectives. Conceivably, one or more of these objectives may be incompatible with the principal strategic aim or with one another. In this case clarification must be sought from the strategic level.

Although maintenance of the aim is a Principle of War, a particular feature of maritime operations is that certain preventive, precautionary or preemptive tasks may be carried

**3.** Army Doctrine
Publication
Volume I: *Operations.*

**4.** Originally applied to
combat by Clausewitz (*On
War*) but now used in an
expanded sense.

**5.** Examples frequently
given are the mass of an
enemy army, the enemies
command structure,
public opinion, national
will, or an alliance or
coalition structure.

out when political, and military strategic, objectives are
unrefined (see Chapter 5 under Naval Diplomacy). Commanders should also be alert to the fact that political objectives can change during the course of a campaign. Indeed
once actual *hostilities* begin, a train of unpredictable events
may be set in hand which will reshape political objectives.
Defining the aim and associated objectives is an iterative
process as the results of operations and new intelligence are
fed back into the decision-making chain.

***Conditions for Success and the End-State.*** In establishing his
aim a commander must consider what constitutes success.
Certain types of task, such as many constabulary tasks, are
ongoing and there will be no easily measurable *conditions for
success.* The same is true for some tasks of naval diplomacy
such as presence. Indeed the only measures of successful
*deterrence* are generally negative. For most *military (or combat
governed) applications of force,* however, success can be defined
as meeting certain specific conditions. These conditions are
referred to in land doctrine as the desired *end-state.*[3] In classical military operations of war, there are usually clear
*military conditions,* such as control of territory, the sea and
airspace, that constitute military success. For *coercive* operations, military conditions often cannot be specified, and
success is measured by compliance or acquiescence by the
target government.

***The Centre of Gravity.*** This expression[4] is used extensively in
land and joint doctrine. The *centre of gravity* can be defined
as that characteristic, capability or location from which
enemy and friendly forces derive their freedom of action,
physical strength or will to fight.[5] There may be both strategic and operational centres of gravity. Success at both the
strategic and operational levels is achieved through identify-
ing and controlling or destroying the enemy's centre of
gravity and protecting one's own. The concept is central to
modern interpretations of *Manoeuvre Warfare* (see Chapter
4). It has not traditionally been a concept of maritime

doctrine[6] but maritime commanders must understand its use in the joint context.

***Critical Vulnerabilities and Systemic Disruption.*** More useful in the maritime environment is the concept of *critical vulnerabilities* which was introduced in Chapter 4 in the context of Manoeuvre Warfare. A critical vulnerability is that part of a force's fighting system which, if destroyed or otherwise neutralised, will lead to *disruption* of the fighting system of that force *(systemic disruption)*. A critical vulnerability may be a concentration of essential *logistics*, a *command and control* installation or an elite force. Disruption may be caused by the physical effects of attack, the psychological effects of coercion or attack, or a mixture of both. In forming his plan an operational commander will look for critical vulnerabilities in his opponent's force structure, should target these if they exist, and attack them when the opportunity arises. He should also be aware of his own critical vulnerabilities and protect them. Critical vulnerability is not, however, a philosopher's stone that, when found, will bring success. Similarly systemic disruption may or may not be achievable. These concepts have primary use in operations where combat is envisaged and likely.

***Decisive Events and Decisive Points.*** The military use of force discussed in Chapter 2 and elsewhere is defined as the use of combat or the threat or possibility of combat, to bring about decisions that will define the subsequent progress of a campaign. A *decisive event* is a military event such as a battle or encounter that defines the course of subsequent events. In a plan that seeks to keep the initiative, a commander will attempt to identify and bring about decisive events on his terms. When the commander can identify decisive events, he should concentrate force to achieve them. The related term *decisive point* is used in land warfare for intermediate objectives, the prosecution of which will provide a marked advantage. They are frequently geographic locations to be seized but may be characteristics or capabilities of the

6. Although the method of achieving *command of the sea* by eliminating the mass of the enemy's fleet in a major sea battle recommended by Mahan suggests the fleet as the centre of gravity, which is close to Clausewitz's original use of the term.

HMS CAMPBELTON
(Type 22) leading the
Standing Naval Force
Atlantic

enemy. They may be multiple and are distinct from the centre of gravity and critical vulnerabilities, although they may provide an avenue to them.

***Cumulative and Sequential Campaigns.*** Campaigns and operations are of two broad types. Campaigns that can be considered as a series of discrete *phases*, each a natural progression and therefore dependent upon the one proceeding it are termed *sequential.* A *cumulative campaign* is one in which the entire pattern of the campaign is made up from a collection of lesser actions, usually independent of each other, offering individual outcomes which together influence the overall outcome of the campaign. The effect is therefore an aggregation or accumulation of these discrete actions. Examples of cumulative campaigns are *guerre de course* (see Chapter 4), a strategic bombing campaign, and some forms of *insurgency*. Cumulative operations may exist within or in parallel to a sequential campaign; for instance, a submarine cumulative operation against the seaborne support of a phased ground campaign. However it is often difficult to predict the timing of success in a cumulative campaign and therefore the timing of the onset of subsequent events.

## Cumulative Campaign in the Second World War

The German and American offensives against merchant shipping in the Second World War were two examples of cumulative campaigns during the Second World War. In both campaigns submarines and aircraft tried to inflict sufficient *attrition* on the enemy merchant fleets so that the vital maritime lines of communication of the Anglo-American alliance and the Japanese Empire would be severed for lack of sufficient ships. Success would be determined by the cumulative effect of a number of otherwise unrelated events. The Germans called this "tonnage warfare". They were unsuccessful in their aim because the introduction and improvement of the convoy system kept Allied losses to bearable levels and eventually led to the defeat of the U-boats. The Japanese only introduced convoy belatedly and did not develop it properly. They thus paid the penalty and lost eighty per cent of their mercantile marine to submarine and air attack. It was a most successful *guerre de course* and it is a matter of debate whether Japan could have continued resistance for long even if nuclear bombs had not been dropped in August 1945.

*Phases of a Sequential Campaign.* In constructing his plan a commander will normally define certain phases of his campaign that will ultimately lead to the desired end-state. As it is not possible to predict in detail the course of events from start to finish, the first phase of a campaign will be subject to the most detailed planning with subsequent phases addressed in outline. Phases may be planned to lead up to a decisive event. Careful consideration of the "what ifs" associated with each phase will greatly enhance the flexibility of a campaign plan. Alternative plans for a particular phase should be considered (*branches*), and planning should be conducted for the possible outcomes of a phase (*sequels*). A campaign may consist of a series of consecutive phases or simultaneous operations or a mixture of both. *Operational pauses* may occur between phases during which logistics can be accumulated, forces rested and reinforcements introduced. Operational pauses may be necessary to avoid reaching a *culminating point.*

### A Sequential Campaign - The Gulf War 1990-91

A good example of a sequential maritime campaign was the maritime contribution to operations against Iraq in 1990-1. The Royal Navy *Task Group* 321.1, part of Operation GRANBY, formed the maritime component of the overall UK Joint Force contribution to Operations DESERT SHIELD and DESERT STORM. First, the Group was closely integrated into the coalition *embargo* effort as it worked itself up for the expected hostilities. The maritime campaign plan was in three phases:

**1.** A progressive sea control campaign consisting of the neutralization of the Iraqi surface fleet and maritime air forces. Sustained sea control, which included RN Type 42 Destroyers providing Anti Air Warfare (AAW) protection well up threat at the northern end of the Gulf, was a prerequisite for subsequent phases. Sea control operations continued during phases 2 and 3 below.

**2.** A maritime contribution to a joint air campaign against Iraq provided by US carriers and cruise missile equipped surface ships and submarines. In this phase the Type 42 Destroyers were an integral part of the US/UK AAW barrier for the coalition maritime forces.

**3.** A move inshore to the Kuwaiti coast with mine countermeasures forces completing the sea control task by clearing the way both for battleships to provide naval gunfire support, and amphibious forces to carry out an assault should it have been required. The Type 42 destroyers provided local area AAW protection to the force and this phase included the shooting down of a Silkworm missile by Seadart.

The war began with an air campaign that was itself initiated with a 72 hour surge (600 carrier sorties per 24 hours) and then continued at a reduced but still rapid *tempo* (400 sorties per 24 hours). Sea control operations continued with the destruction of an initial Iraqi air attack on coalition maritime forces and continued with attacks on Iraqi vessels both in port and at sea. Royal Navy shipborne helicopters were especially successful against Iraqi fast attack craft. Lastly, the third phase, the advance to Kuwait, could be initiated. With the threat to them largely neutralized, mine countermeasures forces were able to clear the way for bombardment and amphibious forces up to the shores of Kuwait. Surface escorts provided protection from the residual threat posed by coastal defence missiles. Fighting ceased before an amphibious landing could take place but the threat of such a landing had an important operational effect. (See Chapter 5 on Combat Operations against the Land).

7. This concept was posited by Clausewitz and is in general use in military doctrine. This meaning is not self-evident as the usual sense of "culmination" is positive and could be associated with success.

*The Culminating Point.*[7] This is the point in time and location when an attacker's *combat power* no longer exceeds that of a defender and he risks effective counter-attack. To be successful, an attack must achieve its objective before reaching a culminating point. Successful defence may involve luring an attacker beyond his culminating point and then counter-attacking. During *linear operations*, the further an attacker advances, the larger the forces that he requires to protect his lengthened lines of support, while the defender may be correspondingly closer to his own logistic bases. Attrition and combat fatigue may also take their toll and contribute to culmination. Another factor that can bring a force to a culminating point is time.

### Risk of Culmination in the Falklands Campaign
During the Falklands Campaign it was important for British forces to have completed the re-occupation before the combined effects of extended lines of support, attrition of forces, possible dwindling of national will, cumulative material defects and the onset of winter might have brought about culmination.

## The Planning Process

Doctrine does not supplant the need for good planning, but it aids the process of thought, and eases the dissemination and understanding of the resulting plan. Furthermore, doctrine, coupled with a clear statement of a *commander's intentions*, allows subordinate commanders to adapt their tactics within a common understanding to achieve their missions in response to a changing situation. In developing his concept of operations the commander must analyze the enemy's situation, vulnerabilities, vital and critical interests and likely courses of action. The situation of his own and friendly forces should be examined along similar lines to that of the enemy. Any restrictions imposed upon the use of force, *Rules of Engagement*, assumptions made and deductions drawn from the analysis must be noted. This analytical process is formalized in the Commander's Estimate, which reviews several courses of action to accomplish a mission, and from which the operational plan can be developed. But such an estimate is only a tool aiding the commander to

Greek M48 tank being embarked into HMS FEARLESS (LPD)

orchestrate the conduct of his campaign or operation. It is not an end in itself. The commander's concept of operations or "design for battle" should serve to exploit his strengths to advantage and ensure that he seizes and maintains the initiative. He should always seek to limit enemy activity to reaction to his own actions thereby ensuring that battles and engagements are fought in the manner, and at the place and time of his choosing. In orchestrating his campaign and designing his battles, the commander must also consider the *Operational Functions*.

Lynx Mk8 at RNAS Portland

## The Operational Functions

These functions have been distilled from historical analysis of maritime operations and are similar to those employed in planning a land campaign. They are:

***Command and Control.*** A maritime operation involves the direction and co-ordination of many activities in all *warfare environments* in what may be a hostile or potentially hostile situation. Command and control must be robust, flexible and capable of dealing with a rapidly changing situation. It must permit swift decision making so that opportunities can be exploited as they are provided. Additionally, it must support the principle of centralized direction and decentralized execution, thus allowing and encouraging freedom of action within the overall concept of operations. Command and control are the subject of Chapter 7.

***Intelligence and Surveillance.*** Success in a campaign is often heavily dependent on the maintenance of a clear picture of the disposition of forces, known at sea as the *Recognized Maritime Picture (RMP)*. Intelligence is an important contributor to this picture, particularly during the early stages of a campaign when it may be necessary to seek political clearance for reconnaissance and intelligence gathering activities. Intelligence is not just a matter of information gathering over the duration of a campaign or operation. Strategic intelligence, which is of more long term significance than operational intelligence or tactical information, is the product of continuous in-depth analysis of the political, economic, industrial and social characteristics of potential adversaries, as well as the military capabilities of any adversary and the characteristics of their armed forces and military leadership. Strategic intelligence is derived from a variety of sources and is used to inform and educate operational intelligence which is more military in focus and specific to the theatre of operations. Operational intelligence needs the political, economic and psychological context for interpretation. Tactical information (sometimes referred to as tactical intelligence) mainly comprises the RMP, and has the narrowest and most detailed military focus. Strategic intelligence, collected over time, enables a commander to use judgement in planning a campaign in the absence of operational intelligence or tactical information, and allows subordinate commanders to act appropriately even when the RMP is sketchy. A commander should nonetheless seek to obtain as much intelligence and information as possible to inform his decision making. On the other hand he should not become a slave to intelligence gathering. There will always be gaps in a commander's knowledge, particularly in the matter of enemy intent, and a commander must be prepared to take decisions in situations of incomplete intelligence. Information that is available must be analyzed, but commanders must be aware of the tendency, present in everyone, to make information fit any preconception.

***Protection.*** The protection of *maritime forces* as an operational function is concerned specifically with preserving the combat power of the force. This can take a variety of forms: layered defence to protect against attack; shielding of high value targets; routeing to avoid enemy capabilities; *deception* to prevent successful enemy attack; and of course the destruction or neutralization of the enemy's combat power. The aim is to preserve one's own power so that it can be used to advantage in the manner, and at the place and time of one's choosing. Methods of protecting a force are discussed in Chapters 4 and 5.

*Application of Combat Power.* The combat power of a maritime force is a combination of its combat systems and ability to bring firepower to bear effectively. Individual units must be given suitable tasks, and commanders the necessary direction so that they can co-ordinate their efforts to execute the concept of operations. All in the command chain must share a common purpose, and personnel must be imbued with the will to fight. Thus leadership and morale, which are discussed in more detail in Chapters 7 and 9, are critical elements of the combat power of a maritime force. A commander should seek to maximize the combat power of his force and then use it to advantage against his enemy. Crucial to success are an accurate assessment of the enemy's strengths and weaknesses, and a correct judgement as to how his own combat power can most effectively be brought to bear against the enemy's critical vulnerability to cause incapacitation or systemic disruption.

*Logistic Support.* The operational function of Logistics is the planning and carrying out of the movement and maintenance of forces. It is both an enabler and a constraint. Good logistic planning is the art of the possible and must be an integral part of operational planning. Logistic considerations pervade all aspects of a campaign from deployment, to employment, and withdrawal. Operational *tempo* cannot be achieved without responsive and reliable logistic resupply. During a campaign logistic support will usually be limited to some degree. Logistic priority must be given to support the *main effort* yet all elements of the force must be adequately provisioned including those engaged in *holding or economy of force operations.* A commander may require to surge his logistic support when the situation demands. Conversely the need to consolidate logistics may be a major factor in planning an operational pause. Logistics are the subject of Chapter 8.

*Influence over the Battlespace.* There is risk associated with any military combat operation. To minimize this risk and ensure success, it is necessary to mould the situation in and around the operating area in order to prevent enemy action from disrupting the operation. This *influence over the battlespace* [8] is achieved by a combination of *command and control warfare* (C2W), control of the electromagnetic spectrum, *interdiction* of enemy forces, and a responsive and agile force capable of acting faster than the enemy. Using these instruments the commander can create the conditions that will allow his operation to succeed. Influence over the battlespace can permit deception, distraction, *disruption*, preemption and *dislocation*. It allows a force to attack the enemy's cohesion and ability to react, whilst simultaneously carrying out operations at a tempo that the enemy cannot match.

These operational functions are not ends in themselves. Rather they assist the commander by allowing him to design his campaign and then execute his concept of operations. The operational functions cannot be viewed separately. They are interdependent and produce a synergy greater than the sum of their individual worth.

## Other Planning Considerations

A commander should also take account of:

*Flexibility.* Plans must be flexible to take account of the unexpected, especially in the light of enemy response.

*Exploitation.* The commander must plan to enhance the strengths of his force and work with the environment while exploiting the opposition's weaknesses.

*A Favourable Balance of Advantage.* The destruction of an enemy's forces will be a deciding factor during combat. In the process own losses must be considered. Society has become less tolerant of the loss of people in combat, both friendly and enemy, and large losses may not be politically acceptable. Furthermore warships are costly, may take weeks to repair and years to replace, while crews take time to train. Preservation of forces will be a factor in planning restricting acceptable risk. To minimize risk, a plan should create the conditions for a highly favourable *balance of advantage* at the decisive event. Calculation of *exchange ratios* should consider both quantitative and qualitative factors.

**Termination.** Termination of a campaign must be considered at the outset of planning. Planning must consider the conditions and the mechanism for withdrawal. Termination of an independent naval operation may be a relatively simple matter compared with that of a fully joint campaign involving extensive *sealift*.

**Organization.** The *task organization* for a campaign must be appropriate to the mission, properly reflect command relationships, and preserve unity of command at the operational and tactical levels (see Chapter 7). Consideration must be given to the scale and experience of staffs and the capacity of headquarters facilities. *Combined* operations bring particular problems as mechanisms must exist for senior officers of national elements to exercise influence in proportion to their contribution, to consult with political authorities, and to provide advice on national capabilities and political constraints.

**Liaison with Civil Authorities.** Close liaison must be maintained with civil authorities in theatre to arrange use of port facilities, diplomatic clearance for passage through *internal waters* and *territorial seas*, staging of aircraft and overflight, control of aircraft movements for the safety of civil aircraft and activation of *Regional Naval Control of Shipping*.

**Public Information.** Images of *conflict* can be brought directly into homes through television, radio and newspapers almost as events are unfolding. The media are a powerful influence on public opinion at home, on an opponent and within the international community. A democratic government can only engage in combat while it has public support and the endorsement or acquiescence of the international community. Although it is possible to exercise some control over the news media at sea, this option must be taken advisedly. Unbalanced reporting can be a consequence of strict control afloat and free reporting from ashore. A commander must treat public information as an important element of his campaign plan so that he can benefit from opportunities and manage negative aspects. A careful balance must be struck between the needs of security and the advantages of candour.

***Biological and Chemical Warfare.*** If the use of Biological and chemical weapons is anticipated then the planning process will need to take account of any constraints this may place on maritime forces, especially in the littoral region.

HMS SLENDID (SSN)

## Mounting a Campaign

In mounting a campaign, the commander will need to co-ordinate all activities leading arrival of the force in theatre ready to achieve a successful outcome. These activities will include:

*Preparation.* Although ships and submarines are stored and manned for combat during peacetime, they are likely to require some additional reprovisioning before they deploy to ensure full stocks are carried. Preparation time will depend on the *readiness* of the unit. Some naval units may require to be brought forward from longer readiness both to provide front line forces and to service any *roulement*. Preparation includes training, both specialist training for a particular environment or task, and group and force training in company. The period of passage into theatre may be used for some *shakedown* and limited *work up* training. However, experience has shown that ships' collective performance can only be effectively honed by appropriately structured staff covered *operational sea training* in a realistic tactical environment .

*Deployment to the Theatre of Operations.* Effective *crisis management* usually demands a rapid response. Force deployment times will vary with the distances involved and speed of transit. Speed and time are not, however, the only considerations in selecting methods of transport. Lead elements of ground forces may be able to deploy into theatre most rapidly by air if suitable airfields and ramp space are available and overflight rights granted, but seaborne transport will usually provide the quickest and invariably the cheapest movement of a substantial force of personnel and equipment.

*Sustainability.* A logistic train may be needed to sustain a campaign and forces using sea lines of support may need protection. See Chapter 8.

**9.** Army Doctrine
Publication
Volume I: *Operations*

# Conducting a Campaign

During the conduct of a campaign or operation a commander should consider:

***Unity of Effort.*** Resources must be concentrated on achieving the aim and should not be squandered on secondary objectives. To achieve this focus a clear statement of the mission and commander's intentions is essential. It may be necessary to designate some operations within a campaign as economy of force or holding operations. Ideally there should be unity of command over all resources including logistics. Where command and control is complex, especially in joint and combined operations, there must be co-operation and co-ordination of activities to this end.

***Tempo.*** Tempo is the rate at which events are driven. Forces that can maintain high tempo, with fast decision-making cycles, can seize the initiative, take advantage of uncertainty, and exploit the weaknesses of the enemy. To achieve high tempo and keep the initiative, and to exploit success an operational commander must be prepared to devolve decision-making. This can be achieved by use of what are sometimes known as *mission orders* that tell a subordinate commander what his task is and its purpose, without dictating how it should be done.

***Simultaneity.***[9] Simultaneity seeks to disrupt the decision making process of the enemy commander by confronting him with a number of problems simultaneously, such as attack or the threat of attack from several directions. He is denied the ability to concentrate on one problem at a time or establish priorities between problems. If simultaneity can be achieved, the enemy's decision making may be delayed or incoherent, allowing the operational commander to seize or maintain the initiative.

***Iterative Planning.*** It is rarely possible to plan in great detail beyond the first phase of a campaign because the outcome of that phase will shape subsequent phases. Part of the planning process must be a consideration of the "what ifs" or branches and sequels. Once the plan has been set in motion, the commander must constantly study the unfolding situation, and revise and reorder the plan as necessary.

### Gallipoli - How not to Fight

The Allied maritime operations in 1915-16 to exploit the possibilities of strategic *leverage* and pass through the Dardanelles with a fleet that would force Turkey out of the war, were a case study in how not to mount a joint operation. The initial plan, to carry out the operation with ships alone, reflected the lack of a joint approach at the *military strategic level*. The original campaign plan underestimated the power of the mutually supporting gun and mine defences, and was finally abandoned because of a failure at the tactical level to neutralize them sufficiently. When amphibious landings on the Gallipoli peninsula eventually took place, inadequacies in command and control resulted in failure to achieve their objectives. There was no doctrine for such operations and tactical commanders did not realize what was expected of them. A second wave of landings failed for the same reasons. The result was stalemate on the ground and the landing forces were eventually withdrawn in a meticulously planned evacuation that was the most successful part of the whole affair. A campaign imaginatively conceived at the *grand strategic level* failed because of strategic, operational and tactical errors.

## The Falklands Campaign - An Illustration

A short account of the campaign to repossess the Falkland Islands in 1982 is at Annex B. This account of a successful maritime campaign illustrates many of the elements of planning discussed in this chapter as well as some of the doctrinal concepts to be found elsewhere in this publication.

# Seven 7

## Command and Control

Effective *Command and Control* (C2), whether it be national, NATO or multinational is fundamental to the efficient employment of *maritime forces.* The successful conduct of operations is dependent on the skilful and timely positioning of forces operating under a clearly defined, yet flexible, command chain. Effective C2 requires resilient high capacity communications

## Definitions

*Command* is the authority granted to an individual to direct, co-ordinate and control military forces. *Control* has two meanings. When used in expressions such as *Operational Control (OPCON)* and *Tactical Control* (TACON), it is the specific level of authority exercised by a commander over organizations not normally under his command. In the expression "Command and Control", "control" means the actual process through which the commander organizes, directs and co-ordinates the activities of forces allocated to him.

RAF GR7 Harriers operating from HMS ILLUSTRIOUS

## Failures of Command and Control at Antwerp

The problems which failures of command and control can bring are well illustrated by the history of British maritime operations against Antwerp. In 1809, in the greatest amphibious operation carried out by Britain to that date, almost 40.000 troops were sent primarily to capture the city and destroy the large French fleet and dockyard and secondly to divert Napoleon from his attack on Austria. The Naval commander, Sir Richard Strachan, did not have the intelligence or doctrinal grasp to operate effectively with the lethargic land force commander Lord Chatham. This resulted in the occupation and eventual evacuation of the island of Walcheren at the mouth of the Scheldt with little else to show for the loss of over 4,000 men, all but 106 to illness. 135 years later in 1944 ineffective operational direction saw the capture of the city of Antwerp totally neutralized by German retention of the Scheldt estuary. Only after a properly carried out maritime operation under effective joint command was Walcheren captured and access to a port, vital to the logistics of the Allied armies, obtained.

# Higher Command of the Armed Forces

The command of each of the United Kingdom's fighting Services is vested in the Sovereign. The Secretary of State for Defence (SofS) is appointed by the Crown after nomination by the Prime Minister and is accountable to Parliament. SofS who is responsible for the defence of the realm, is supported by the Defence Council, and is advised by the Chief of the Defence Staff (CDS). The Service Chiefs of Staff are members of the Defence Council and are individually responsible for the fighting effectiveness, management, overall efficiency and morale of their respective Services. They report to the Secretary of State through the CDS, but retain the right of direct access to the Secretary of State and the Prime Minister.

1. A Permanent Joint Headquarters is to be established at Northwood, Middlesex, in 1996.

2. Particularly those between the Ministry of Defence (policy and strategic direction of an operation) and the Joint Headquarters (the conduct of an operation).

## Organization

For United Kingdom national operations overall command is exercised by the CDS. Most future *campaigns* and operations are likely to be joint, that is, involve more than one Service. CDS will therefore appoint a *Joint Commander (JC)*. The Jt Comd exercises Operational Command (OPCOM) over the forces assigned to him at a Joint Headquarters.[1] In theatre, a *Joint Force Commander (JFC)* will be nominated, and he will exercise *Operational Control (OPCON)* through the individual component commanders. This organization provides the essential unity of command required at the operational level. It also ensures that authority and responsibility[2] for an operation are clearly defined, and appropriate expertise and experience is in place to provide effective command and control of assigned forces. This structure requires a trained and experienced joint staff

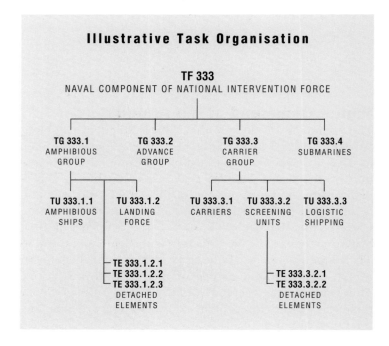

### Illustrative Task Organisation

**TF 333**
NAVAL COMPONENT OF NATIONAL INTERVENTION FORCE

| **TG 333.1** AMPHIBIOUS GROUP | **TG 333.2** ADVANCE GROUP | **TG 333.3** CARRIER GROUP | **TG 333.4** SUBMARINES |
|---|---|---|---|

| **TU 333.1.1** AMPHIBIOUS SHIPS | **TU 333.1.2** LANDING FORCE | **TU 333.3.1** CARRIERS | **TU 333.3.2** SCREENING UNITS | **TU 333.3.3** LOGISTIC SHIPPING |
|---|---|---|---|---|

TE 333.1.2.1
TE 333.1.2.2
TE 333.1.2.3
DETACHED ELEMENTS

TE 333.3.2.1
TE 333.3.2.2
DETACHED ELEMENTS

drawn from the participating Services and Branches. This in turn necessitates regular exercises in joint command and control. Levels of command are illustrated in Figure 7.1.

Centralized direction must, however, be combined with decentralized execution, as tactical considerations are generally best left to the on scene commander. Effective command and control must therefore comprise direction at the highest level necessary to achieve unity of purpose, combined with the delegation of responsibility for achieving objectives to the lowest level commensurate with the most appropriate and effective use of resources.

*Task Organization.* Maritime forces are organized *functionally* for operations into a *task organization* consisting of a maximum of four levels of *echelonment: task forces, task groups, task units* and *task elements.* The use of these levels is flexible and they bear no direct relationship to levels of command or levels of planning. United Kingdom and NATO task forces are given three digit designators and the numbering of the subordinate formations include one, two or three decimal points to illustrate the command relationship between the formations. The size and content of these formations are entirely dependent on the needs of the particular campaign or operation. A task element would typically contain fewer than ten units. An illustrative task organization is shown in the box above.

## Multinational Operations

In NATO or other coalition operations with forces from more than one country, multinational aspects will create an additional dimension to the command and control organization. *Combined* operations, that is, those that are conducted by *integrated* multinational forces, are complex. They involve forces with different national equipment and *doctrine,* often with specific political constraints on their employment. Close liaison between the various governments and their own individual services is required to ensure the

HMS HERALD
acting as a MCM
Command Platform
to a multinational
MCM group during the
Gulf War (1992)

achievement of common objectives. When national forces are assigned to a NATO operation, OPCOM and OPCON will normally be given to a *Major NATO Commander (MNC)*. The NATO chain of command has traditionally passed from MNC through a *Major Subordinate Commander (MSC)* and *Principal Subordinate Commander (PSC)* to the operational formations. Following the introduction of the *Combined Joint Task Force (CJTF)* Concept, a CJTF Commander may be appointed under the command of an MNC or MSC. He will normally have OPCON of all the different participating national units. The CJTF Concept can also be used for purely European operations under WEU command, and also for operations in which other nations participate alongside NATO or WEU forces.

***Degrees of Operational Co-operation of Multinational Forces.*** While command structures within NATO are formalized, those for coalition operations outside NATO will depend on the political objectives and legal constraints of coalition partners and the capabilities and *interoperability* of their forces. There are several degrees of integration that might be achieved. Indeed more than one degree may coexist in a single campaign or operation.

***Full Integration or Combination.*** Forces of more than one nation operate under a single *unified* command structure. Full integration requires a high degree of interoperability normally only achieved within a formal alliance. *Rules of Engagement* must be completely *harmonized* (preferably using a single system) and there must be formal systems for achieving multinational consensus over political and military objectives at the *grand strategic* and *military strategic levels.* There may be a need for national missions or liaison staffs at the *operational level.* NATO operations are normally conducted with fully integrated forces.

***Co-ordination.*** The forces of more than one nation or coalition operate to achieve shared objectives in a single theatre. There may not be a formal unified command structure but there will probably be informal multinational arrangements in theatre at the operational level. These arrangements will allow forces to share common tasks, prevent mutual interference, and, at higher levels, to identify and define shared objectives and common courses of action. Rules of engagement should be harmonized although this may not be possible. In any event each national force should be aware of the levels of ROE *permission and prohibition* under which other nations are operating. Maritime forces frequently cooperate in this way.

**3.** Concertation was used in WEU papers to describe the degree of cooperation between some WEU forces during the Gulf War and the Iran/Iraq War.

Watchkeeping in a submarine Control Room

***Basic Co-operation*** (*Concertation*[3]). Forces of friendly nations sharing similar interests operate in a single theatre of operations. Common policy objectives have not been defined but there is agreement (possibly informal) to provide some mutual assistance and to deconflict activities. Rules of engagement are unlikely to be harmonized but it is beneficial to know the general extent of other nations' ROE permissions and prohibitions. Although no formal co-ordination structures exist in theatre, there may be liaison between diplomatic missions, exchanges of military liaison officers, and ad hoc operational or tactical level military meetings.

## Communications

Effective communication links, particularly secure, are essential to successful command and control. Interoperability of communications equipment is especially important in joint and combined operations. Despite progress in commonality within NATO, the level of sophistication of communications equipment varies between countries and this will have an impact on the way in which control is exercised. Certain ships may require more comprehensive communications fits to meet the C2 needs of a force.

Global communications and modern data transmission systems have enabled command and control to be effected many thousands of miles from the theatre of action. Although modern equipment has increased the amount of information available to the commander, it has also significantly reduced the time available for decision making. A well trained staff is necessary to filter very large amounts of information. This staff needs to be frequently exercised in processing, analyzing and despatching information quickly and accurately using an appropriate support system.

No commander should be wholly dependent on an umbilical communications link with higher command

Landing Force HQ ashore supported by specialist amphibious shipping

Royal Marines
disembarking from a
Seaking MK4

ashore or afloat. It is essential, therefore, that commanders and their staffs have a clear understanding of the higher commanders' intentions so that they can take appropriate action in the absence of timely direction. This requirement reinforces the importance of decentralized execution. At the operational level such understanding should include appreciation of national policy and the diplomatic and political environment in which operations are being conducted. As a general rule a commander and his staff should understand their immediate superior's detailed intentions, and the broad intentions of the commander two levels above him. The related subject of *mission orders* is discussed in Chapter 6.

The command and control systems of a command ship and the intelligence systems and communications connectivity supporting them are elaborate and comprehensive. They are strategically and operationally highly mobile, and allow joint control at the operational level to be exercised over a large theatre of operations.

## Rules of Engagement

In operations across the *spectrum of conflict*, Rules of Engagement (ROE) are issued to provide political direction, guidance and instruction to commanders. ROE are the primary means of defining political limits to the use of military force and take the form of prohibitions and permissions. They can be instruments of both *escalation* and *de-escalation*. They are formulated and sought by military staffs at the operational and tactical levels and authorized at the political (grand strategic) level following further miliary advice at the military strategic level. ROE must be continually revised to reflect changing military and political circumstances. Dormant ROE may be prepared and authorized for use if certain contingencies arise. It is a military strategic level function of the very greatest importance to ensure that ROE are crafted to allow effective use of military force, while providing proper protection. The operational commander in turn must ensure that he fully understands these rules, promulgates them throughout his force and is willing to make a robust case for alterations when circumstances change. It is a major challenge to create in a few words a vivid and succinct description of the changing situation, possible outcomes, and precise reasons for seeking new or amended rules. Consequently adequate time and training will be needed for ROE at all levels of military planning. Rules of Engagement are likely to be significant planning constraints and may restrict the choice of what would otherwise be appropriate courses of action.

During multinational operations variations in national ROE may be a principal constraint on the tasking of forces (See Multinational Operations above).

## Space

Modern command and control makes extensive use of space systems for communications and navigational accuracy, as well as important strategic and operational uses for surveillance. The United States is a principal contributor of space systems to Alliance and coalition operations. Space is one of the five *warfare environments*.[4] It can be an important enabler but may equally be exploited by a sophisticated opponent.

## Command and Control Warfare

Effective Command and Control is essential to success in modern operations. Protection and maintenance of C2 facilities is of paramount importance since the whole system can be degraded through the loss or malfunctioning of one, or a small number of, components. Consequently operations conducted against an opponent's C2 infrastructure play a key part in modern *conflict*. In recognition of the importance of the battle for control of information, the term *Command and Control Warfare (C2W)* has been devised to embrace some aspects of *electronic warfare*, destruction, *deception, psychological operations* and *operational security* under one composite warfare discipline. C2W aims at denying information to an enemy, exploiting, influencing, degrading, confusing or destroying the enemy C2 capabilities, and protecting friendly C2 against such actions. Good intelligence and co-ordination between various elements in joint and combined forces are essential to the success of C2W.

## Command and Leadership

Effective command depends on effective leadership. Born leaders are rare, but leadership potential can be developed by training, experience, study of the methods of great leaders in the past, and a knowledge of military doctrine. Through this process an individual must develop his[5] own style of leadership. No two people can, or should, lead in exactly the same way.

*Use of Doctrine.* Commanders must have a clear grasp of current *doctrine* so that they can fully comprehend their orders and execute them effectively. A knowledge of doctrine will also allow commanders to take decisions in

On watch in a surface
ship's Operations Room

accordance with the intentions of their superiors even when
they are out of contact with higher levels of command.
Commanders must, however, use judgement. They must not
follow doctrine slavishly but must learn from the lessons of
their own experience and be prepared to deviate from
established doctrine when required, explaining their
reasons for doing so to their subordinates.

139

### Qualities for Leadership

The development of leadership potential involves study of
the qualities of others and must start with self discipline. It
is a continuous process throughout training and daily life. It
is the prime responsibility of all leaders to promote this
process amongst their subordinates by:

- precept and example;

- advice, encouragement and admonishment;

- giving subordinates every opportunity of leading.

### The Nelson Touch

One of Nelson's great strengths as a commander was his confident
willingness to amend established doctrine when necessary. Before
Trafalgar he explained, as he put it, "not only to the commanders of
the fleet but almost to every individual" how he was going to deviate
from the standard single line of battle. That deployment would not
obtain as decisive results as a more daring ploy. Recognising that the
weaknesses of the French and Spanish were cumbersome and
inflexible command and control and poor gunnery tactics and
expertise, he decided to approach the enemy line in two perpendicular
lines of his own to cut it into three sections that could be annihilated in
detail. " ...it was like an electric shock. Some shed tears. All approved -
it was new - it was singular - it was simple!" (Lord Nelson (1758 -
1805) in a letter to Lady Hamilton dated 1 Oct 1805). His captains put
the plan into effect to achieve the greatest victory in the Royal Navy's
history.

An outstanding characteristic of all great commanders is
their refusal to be dominated by circumstances. While not
challenging the inevitable, they use events around them to
achieve their own ends, rather than modify their ends to
keep pace with the tide of events. Personal qualities present
in a great commander are:-

- the ability to grasp the essentials important to success;

- firmness and speed in decision, largely acquired by thinking out during quiet periods what action should be taken if different circumstances arise;

- calmness in crisis; the courage to withstand mental stress and strain, and the refusal to be distracted by bad tidings;

- the ability to explain clearly what he wants to achieve and why, so that he can be effectively and appropriately supported by his peers and subordinates;

- boldness; a good leader must be successful to retain the confidence of his subordinates, and success will not come from faintheartedness;

- a readiness to accept and discharge responsibility at all times; the mere acceptance of responsibility without the determination to fulfil it by executive action is useless;

- the ability to generate mutual trust, respect and confidence between himself and subordinates, peers and superiors.

- the ability to convince subordinates at all levels that he has their best interests at heart by a mixture of wide and sympathetic understanding of human nature (supported by a sense of humour), an understanding of the strengths and weaknesses of individuals, and meticulous and impartial care in dealing with their affairs.

- the ability to listen to and learn from others and to make full use of their particular talents and expertise.

- the confidence to delegate in the knowledge that his intentions have been clearly expressed and well promulgated.

### The Failure to Delegate

The history of the Royal Navy in the Twentieth Century is littered with officers who perverted their natural instincts for hard work into gross over centralization. This led to such disasters as the scattering and subsequent massacre of Convoy PQ17 on the personal orders of a First Sea Lord who did not have a clear understanding of the tactical situation. Similarly officers have worked themselves to premature deaths. The other side of this coin, an unwillingness to act on initiative in an over- centralised Grand Fleet, was a major factor in the escape of the Germans from almost certain destruction after the Battle of Jutland in 1916.

## Combat Stress and Fatigue

Every commander must know how hard to drive his force. It must not be spurred beyond the limits at which both personnel and machines loose their powers of recovery. Undue mental strain often leads to physical exhaustion and undue physical strain to mental eccentricities. Combat stress is inherent in warfare but it can be tempered by an individual's physical and moral courage and by his confidence in a sound and well-expressed plan. A commander must have a firm knowledge of the dangers and warning signs of unrelieved combat stress. Effective leadership, self-control and confidence in the team all combine to help limit the natural fear of violence.

A commander must also consider his own fatigue, for it is essential that his energy, mental and physical, should be conserved for crucial periods. He must ensure he has adequate and regular periods of rest and reflection, avoid over-immersion in matters of detail that are the job of his staff and delegate as much as possible to subordinates. He should issue clear and concise orders and leave his staff to work out the details. This creates a more responsive force, gives subordinates vital experience essential for their own development and preserves the vital force of the commander for when it is most required.

# NATIONAL LEVELS OF COMMAND

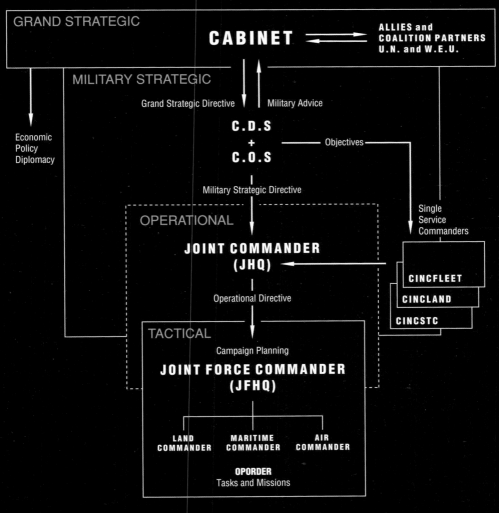

GRAND STRATEGIC

**CABINET** ⇄ **ALLIES and COALITION PARTNERS U.N. and W.E.U.**

MILITARY STRATEGIC

Grand Strategic Directive | Military Advice

Economic Policy Diplomacy

**C.D.S + C.O.S** —— Objectives ——

Military Strategic Directive

Single Service Commanders

OPERATIONAL

**JOINT COMMANDER (JHQ)** ⟵

**CINCFLEET**
**CINCLAND**
**CINCSTC**

Operational Directive

TACTICAL

Campaign Planning

**JOINT FORCE COMMANDER (JFHQ)**

**LAND COMMANDER** | **MARITIME COMMANDER** | **AIR COMMANDER**

**OPORDER**
Tasks and Missions

Figure 7.1

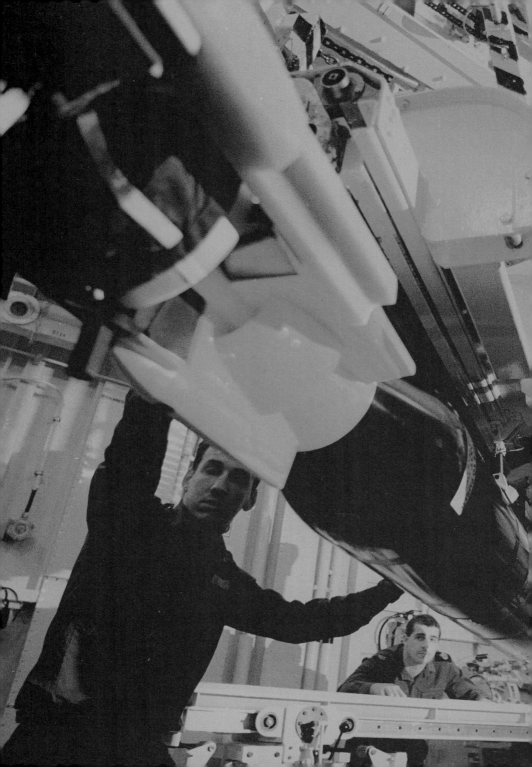

# *Eight* 8

## Maritime Logistics and Support

Logistics play an important part in determining a nation's capacity to sustain *war*. The control, distribution and availability of *materiel* will directly influence the *tempo*, shape and outcome of any *campaign*.

## Maritime Logistics
## in the Joint Environment

The purpose of logistic support is to ensure the provision, sustainment and recovery of forces at the required level for the duration of operations. Logistic support includes medical and repair facilities, movement of personnel, and the transport of the fuel, lubricants ordnance, spare parts, food and other provisions, and the many stores required for combat. The sea has overwhelming advantages as a transport medium for large, heavy and bulky items. Ships are, therefore, important *joint* logistic assets. The availability of shipping may thus ultimately govern whether, where and when operations can take place ashore. As a corollary, however, the use of sea lines of support to a campaign may be a *critical vulnerability*, so shipping may require protection. Similarly, at the tactical level, a formation's *organic* logistic shipping will almost invariably be essential to its mission and thus require special effort to be devoted to its defence.

A Spearfish torpedo being loaded into HMS TRENCHANT (SSN)

**Field Marshal Viscount Alanbrooke's Appreciation of Sea Transport's Importance in the Second World War**

"Brooke's strategy, like that of all Britain's greatest commanders, depended on salt water. With his grasp of essentials, he saw that sea transport was the key to the offensive. Without it nothing could be done to take the pressure off Russia or deprive the enemy, with his central land position, of the initiative." Sir Arthur Bryant from The Turn of the Tide 1939-1943: A study based on the Diaries and Autobiographical Notes of Field Marshal The Viscount Alanbrooke KG OM. Field Marshal Alanbrooke (1883-1963), formerly Sir Alan Brooke, was Chief of the Imperial General Staff and Chairman of the Chiefs of Staff Committee from 1941 to 1945 and is regarded as a master of strategy. Churchill too wrote: "Shipping was at once the stranglehold and sole foundation of our war strategy." The Second World War Volume IV. (Reproduced with permission of Curtis Brown Ltd, London on behalf of the Estate of Sir Winston S Churchill. Copyright the Estate of Sir Winston S Churchill.)

The ability of ships to carry and transfer stores and fuel gives modern *maritime forces* a unique potential for self sustained operations at considerable distances from fixed bases. Indeed the sailor is so used to the level of organic logistic support that is provided routinely in a ship and tactical formation that logistic considerations have not had the apparent significance at the tactical level that they have to the soldier. On land the availability and security of logistic support is a concern even for the lowest level of command. For the operational commander, however, maritime and land logistics are not conceptually dissimilar, as the ability to use lines of support along which a maritime force is *consolidated*, is directly comparable to tasks relating to seaborne support of land operations and to land lines of support. In any event logistic support is fundamentally a joint activity in which resources and facilities must be pooled to the utmost extent possible between Services. It is a tenet of joint

1. JSP1  *doctrine* that administrative services of common usage in the three Services should be provided by one Service for the use of others.[1] At the operational level, joint aspects of logistic policy, planning and execution will predominate.

## Planning and Control of Logistics

*Logistics at the Grand and Military Strategic Levels (Production and Consumer Logistics).* At the grand strategic level logistics provide a bridge between the economy of a nation and the operations of combat forces. The creation of logistic resources (production logistics) is largely a civilian commercial process. The monitoring, development and sustainment of production capability in a nation's industrial base is an important aspect of *reconstitution* planning. The employment of these resources in support of combat forces (consumer logistics) is a military function, although heavily dependent on civilian support. The integration of production and consumer logistic systems takes place at the *military strategic level* in the Defence Staff and, for the *Naval Service*, in the Naval Support Command and the Controllerate of the Navy. The determination of strategic requirements, procurement, planning of logistic aspects of *regeneration*

RFA's FORT GEORGE
(AOR) and
BLACK ROVER (AOL)
in company with
HMS ARGYLL (Type 23)

capability, central storage and bulk distribution are all military strategic logistic functions.

***Logistics at the Operational Level.*** Operational logistic functions are: the movement of logistics into, within and out of theatre; the establishment of logistic bases; the apportionment and allocation of logistics between subordinate commands; and the protection of logistics bases, on land, and *along lines of support*. In war, protection of logistics may constitute a major operation or campaign in its own right. A commander must ensure that his logistic plan is adequate to support his concept of operations. Logistic feasibility will frequently be the deciding factor in choosing a course of action. For this reason logistic planning will require the same attention as planning for warfighting, and must underpin all envisaged contingencies during each phase of the campaign plan. This process is aided if the commander at each level has control over the allocation of the logistic support to forces under his command. Complete unity of logistic command is desirable but difficult to achieve for two principal reasons. First, the harmonization of production and consumer logistics is a continuous process involving a large number of organizations most of whom will not be under the control of the operational commander. He may therefore have little control of the supply side of his logistics. Secondly there are particular problems associated with the control of logistics during multinational operations. The establishment of a *Component Commander* subordinate to the Joint Force Commander with responsibility for logistic support will enhance unity of logistic command in national joint operations.

***Multinational Logistics.*** Logistics during multinational operations have traditionally been a national responsibility. This will inevitably be the case within an ad hoc coalition where there is little standardization between nations' equipments. However NATO and the WEU have developed a principle of collective responsibility between member nations and Allied

SeaKing MK6 (ASW) helicopter with an underslung load

2. JSP1   authorities for *combined* operations. Allied maritime contingency planning includes the establishment of a *Multinational Logistic Support Commander (MNLC)* to plan, co-ordinate and control all maritime logistic shore support for MNMFs. Interoperability within an alliance is a prerequisite if one nation's logistic resources are to support another's, and considerable work in NATO's standardization agencies is devoted to this end. Standardization of fuel grades, replenishment rigs and connections allow for regular transfer of fuel between NATO nations, and indeed between other nations who have adopted NATO standards. Medical support, supply of provisions and general stores, and non-specialist transport can generally be treated as common resources. Although NATO and the WEU have developed plans and procedures for the co-ordination of logistic support in combined operations, specific national requirements, especially in ammunition resupply and the maintenance and repair of weapon systems, still limit the effectiveness of combined logistics.

*Logistic Principles.* The principles of joint logistics are: foresight, economy, flexibility, simplicity and co-operation.[2] The need for foresight in logistic planning has been discussed earlier in this chapter, as has the requirement for coopera-

Amphibious logistic support being transfered ashore on a Mexeflote

tion between Services, nations and commands particularly where control of logistics is not unified. Economy, flexibility and simplicity deserve special mention:

*Economy.* Logistics resources will usually be in short supply and sufficiency should be the objective of the logistician. It is possible to overplan as well as to underplan logistic requirements. Overplanning can consume resources that could be devoted to combat forces. Furthermore, an over large logistic organization may require additional logistics staff who, in turn, will need logistic support, and the whole may draw forces for protection away from the main effort.

RFA FORT GRANGE
(AFSH) on passage

*Flexibility.* A logistic plan must be flexible and capable of responding to inevitable changes in the operational plan. Equally the logistic system that executes the plan must be capable of adapting to rapid changes of requirement. A large logistics organization geared to supporting a major campaign can acquire a momentum of its own and generate wasteful stockpiles of materiel if it is not sensitive to change. It may also be necessary for an operational commander to take a calculated risk over logistic sufficiency, in particular where there are opportunities to exploit success or to maintain tempo. For example, he may allow the fuel and ammunition levels of a *naval force* that is exploiting success to fall below prudent norms in the expectation that consolidation forces will arrive. A flexible logistic system will minimize differences between operational and logistic tempo and therefore the attendant risk. It is relevant that a principal reason for the planning of *operational pauses* in a campaign is to allow the consolidation of logistics and to avoid reaching *culmination* before success is achieved (See Chapter 6 for discussions of the culminating point and tempo).

*Simplicity.* Any unnecessarily complicated aspect of operational planning will be prone to disruption. Logistic planning is in large part carried out by experts and can appear intractable to non-experts charged with assessment and

HMS ARGYLL (Type 23)
entering a covered dock
at Devonport

execution. The principal non-expert may be the operational commander. A comprehensive, but simple, plan that accords with the direction given by the operational commander is more likely to gain approval and to be correctly interpreted and executed.

## Roulement

Consideration must be given at an early stage in strategic and operational planning to relieving maritime forces which remain in an operational theatre for an extended period. Although ships, given sufficient logistic support, can remain on station almost indefinitely, the efficiency of personnel can be expected to decline during deployment. Furthermore, training in tasks and functions not directly connected with the mission may suffer, as may some aspects of maintenance if the tempo of operations is high. The rotation of ships and personnel on station to maintain a high state of *readiness* is known as *roulement* and is an important feature of the maritime component of a campaign plan.

## Shore Support

Shore support provides the starting point for any maritime logistic chain. The home base will provide the main supply depots and dockyard facilities. Most supplies and repairs are obtained from the private sector under contract. Procurement of materiel must be carefully monitored both to ensure that adequate stocks of equipment and stores are available for transfer to the fleet and to avoid wasting resources in the production and retention of unnecessarily large stocks.

When *Host Nation Support (HNS)* is available, it may supplement afloat support by providing useful forward airheads for logistic and personnel movements to and from the theatre of operations, and forward operating bases for replenishment, maintenance and repair. HNS may help to economize on the need for logistics, but such support is not an essential feature of purely maritime operations. Indeed a forward operating base may be no more than a sheltered anchorage for a support or repair ship. However once troops are ashore, the significance and dimensions of the organization to co-ordinate and take advantage of HNS can increase substantially. HNS arrangements are often preplanned in outline and formalized by inter-governmental Memoranda of Understanding (MOU). They are, nevertheless, not guaranteed to remain in force as the situation changes.

## Sustained Reach

Royal Fleet Auxiliary Afloat support gives maritime forces unique capabilities to carry out sustained operations at considerable distances from their home base. Replenishment at Sea (RAS) from *auxiliary* ships enables naval forces to extend their *reach* world wide without the need to enter port. The United Kingdom continues to maintain its considerable investment in these ships. Although an integral part of the Fleet, the Royal Navy's logistic shipping is organized as the *Royal Fleet Auxiliary (RFA)*, manned by personnel employed under Merchant Navy articles. No British maritime force is complete without its RFAs to provide fuel and other stores, and RFA officers provide afloat support expertise on command staffs. In *crisis*, the RFA can be augmented by *Ships Taken Up From Trade (STUFT)* for the *lift* of troops and materiel. The mechanisms for taking ships up from trade are well established and early identification of the need for STUFT is important if forces containing STUFT are to be formed in a timely fashion.

### The Maritime Operational Logistics Pipeline

The sustained reach of maritime forces, and the reach which they in turn provide to other forces, is a key attribute of maritime power. However military and RFA support shipping form only a part of the maritime logistic system. Figure 8.1 shows the extent of the Operational Logistics Pipeline from the UK bases to the furthest forward fighting unit. The Pipeline includes an initial *Handling* Point (HP1), a possible *Advanced Logistic Support Site (ALSS)* and potentially several *Forward Logistics Sites (FLS)* within the operational theatre. The establishment and maintenance of these sites, together with the provision of transport between them, will in most cases be a joint and frequently multinational requirement. The locations of the ALSS and FLS would be chosen to provide optimal support to the campaign, which may need to move if the situation changes.

The pipeline must handle the movement of material and people into, within and from the operational area. Personnel may include casualties, refugees, displaced persons and prisoners of war. Segments of the pipeline may consist of air, land or sea transport, which could be supporting all three Services as well as multinational requirements. Priorities across commodities, services and nations will need to be established to cater for constraints on transport capacity.

## Conclusion

The careful preparation of logistics in peacetime and the building of confidence between logisticians and warfare specialists at each level of command, is fundamental to the success of operational logistics in crisis and war. Warfare and logistics are inseparable partners in maritime operations.

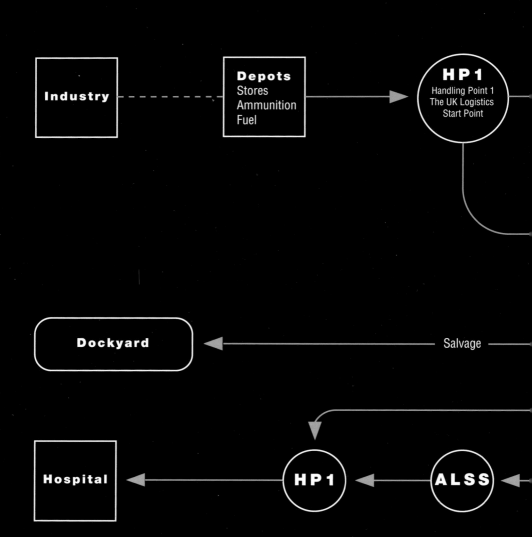

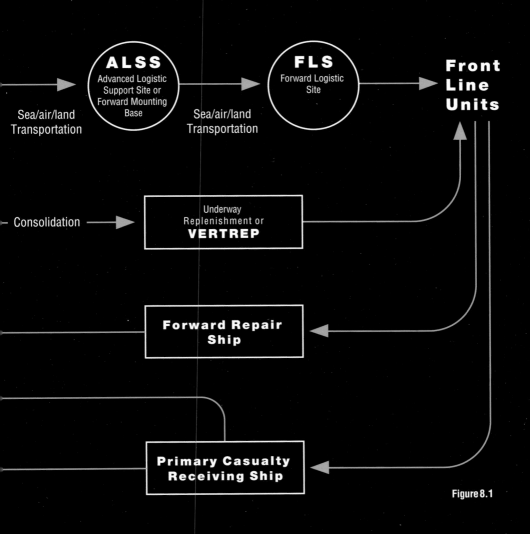

Figure 8.1

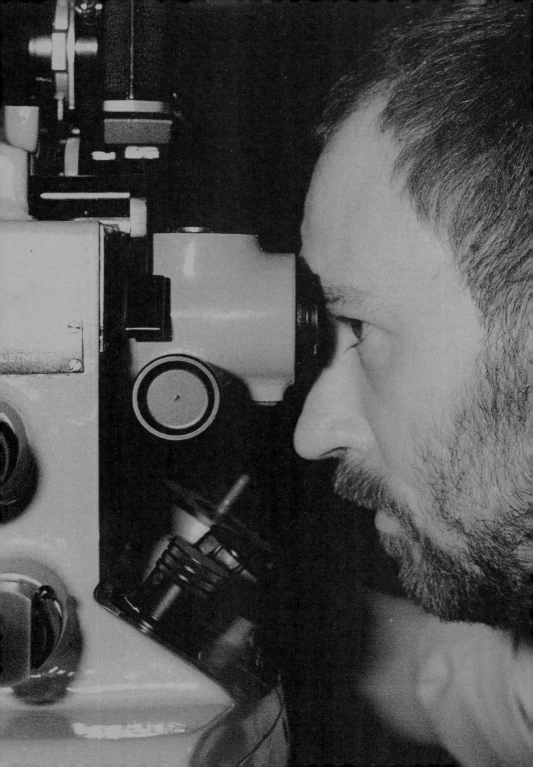

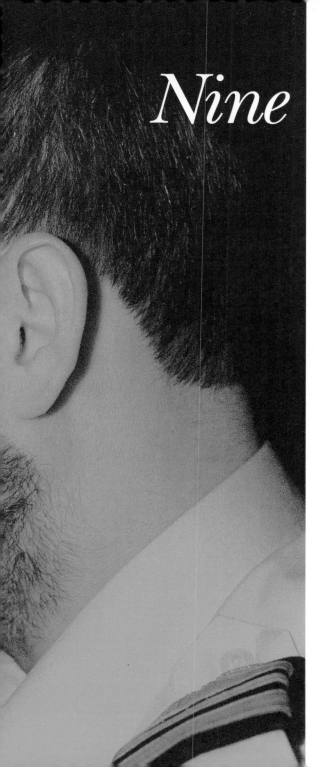

# *Nine* 9

## Maritime Combat Capabilities

The applications discussed in Chapter 5 encompass a wide range of operational situations from peacetime activities to full *hostilities*. The majority are *military (combat governed)*. It is the ability to continue action through to combat if necessary, or the message maritime forces convey, that confers on them effectiveness in a military sense.

## Introduction

Although the United Kingdom's Defence Policy envisages that major operations would normally be conducted alongside our NATO and WEU allies or in ad hoc coalition with other friendly nations, the national requirements of *Defence Roles* 1 and 3 require the maintenance of a balanced, independent maritime capability. Such maritime capabilities contribute to the overall capability of Allied or coalition formations during *combined* operations.

Seaking Mk6 (ASW) and
Seaking Mk2 (AEW)
approaching to land on
HMS ARK ROYAL (CVS)

***National Considerations.*** The United Kingdom needs to be able to field *National Contingency Forces* for those occasions when we operate alone. A balanced national force will be composed of ships, aircraft and ground units each bringing specific capabilities necessary to execution of a particular mission without excessive redundancy.

***Multinational Considerations.*** It is not possible to create robust coalition formations capable of high intensity combat at short notice from an assembly of disparate national capabilities. *Maritime forces* can easily be brought together to form a multinational force for tasks in which there is a low risk of combat. However, a fully integrated fighting force requires a period to work up from basic levels of inter-operability to full operational capability under the direction of an experienced commander and afloat staff. Within NATO the problem of creating major multinational fighting formations is simplified because it is probable that the United States will provide the core capabilities for a *NATO Task Force* or *NATO Expanded Task Force*. For a WEU or other coalition operation in which the US has chosen not to participate with combat forces, these core capabilities must be provided by other nations. The United Kingdom, as a leading European maritime nation, would be able to make a significant contribution in the allocation of forces to such an operation. In these circumstances the UK is one of very few nations that could provide the core building blocks, such as a carrier task group and amphibious force, to a multinational formation. It can also contribute a proven, comprehensive command and control capability. Furthermore, the ability to contribute a major combat formation to a coalition will secure an effective voice in how national forces are used in a multinational operation. Degrees of integration of multinational forces are discussed in Chapter 7.

***The Balanced Fleet.*** There are therefore both national and multinational reasons for the United Kingdom to possess a spread of maritime assets each with a distinctive range of combat capabilities, in other words a *balanced fleet*. Independent national operations require the complete suite of maritime warfare capabilities (discussed in this chapter) at both the operational and tactical levels. For coalition operations a balanced fleet will enable the UK to make an effective contribution to multinational formations, thereby endorsing our authority.

*Readiness.* In a strategic environment in which there is likely to be extensive warning of major attack but in which other crises may develop with little warning, realistic but prudent force readiness is a complex matter of fundamental strategic importance. National *readiness* levels are designed in part to service NATO force structures (described in Chapter One). However for *naval forces*, the cycle of refit, trials, operational sea training, operations and maintenance periods dictates that a proportion of units will be at longer readiness to provide a roulement for those at short readiness. It follows that changes in the strategic requirement for Main Defence and Augmentation forces do not in themselves alter the requirement for a proportion of naval forces to be at longer readiness.

This chapter surveys the range of maritime capabilities required to conduct combat operations against a competent enemy with a modern order of battle. The maritime component of an independent national *intervention* campaign is used to illustrate these capabilities and their contribution to the governing *operational functions* of *command and control*, intelligence, protection, *application of combat power*, *logistic support* and *influence over the battlespace* that were introduced in Chapter 6. The relative importance of these functions will vary during the different stages of a campaign. As a gross simplification there are seven stages that can be identified: identification of a *crisis*; force generation; deployment; *sea control* operations; *power projection*; support to operations ashore; and withdrawal. In reality these stages will not be easily distinguishable; nor will they necessarily coincide with the *phases* of a specific campaign plan. This chapter highlights the most significant operational functions in each of the stages but does not dwell on their nuances for which operational level doctrinal and planning publications should be consulted. Following this discussion of the stages of a maritime campaign, there is a summary of the contributions of individual maritime vessels, aircraft and amphibious units. The most important single factor in a *Naval Service* is the quality of its personnel and their training. The chapter concludes on this theme.

## Identification of a Crisis

Initial indications that a crisis is developing will probably come from a variety of sources including strategic intelligence, wide area *surveillance* systems, and informal sources such as the news media. Intelligence gathering and analysis can provide warning of changes in operating patterns, exercise and *workup* programmes and communications volume, and allow for *strategic level* identification and evaluation of potential crises. Intelligence recovery is now a global science which involves close co-operation with allies, swift dissemination of assessed data, clear presentation and early background advice to commanders. Early assessment of the military capability of any potential adversary will play a significant part in assessment of the size and composition of forces needed to address a crisis.

Maritime forces operating offshore in international waters can gather a wide variety of useful intelligence and provide a significant surveillance capability. Information gathered in this way is sometimes the only reliable source of evidence, and as such is a critical element in identification and assessment of the a crisis. Monitoring of shipping or air activity may be a preliminary phase to embargo or sanctions enforcement or may support other constabulary tasks such as drug interdiction.

Intelligence gathering and surveillance will continue

throughout a campaign, although its focus will shift from the strategic and general in the early stages to the operational and tactical and hence become more specifically military as the campaign develops.

## Force Generation

The size and composition of the forces required to respond to a developing crisis will be shaped by:

- the policy objectives and strategic concept - what the Government wants to achieve, how it wishes to act and, in a multinational operation, what the United Kingdom contribution should be;

- understanding of the military *conditions for success or end-state* - what the military commander must achieve to be successful;

- assessment of the threat - and therefore the combat power and levels of protection that may be required;

- the forces available - which will depend in part on the priority given by Government to the policy objectives;

- the time available to respond.

Among the factors that must be considered are: the need for a robust, flexible, and responsive command and control system able to adapt to changing force levels and threat and, in multi-national operations, meet any national requirements; the potential duration of the campaign, and the need to sustain or increase force levels; and logistic support to the force throughout the campaign. Preparation of forces is discussed in Chapter 6 under "Mounting a Campaign".

## Deployment

Deployment to a theatre of operations involves: mounting and sailing the force from home bases (although maritime forces can often be diverted directly from their current locations); passage to the area of operations; transit; and arrival in the theatre of operations in a posture appropriate to the threat and mission. Co-ordination of the deployment will require detailed planning, close liaison with diplomatic posts, other civil authorities, Allied military authorities and probably foreign government agencies. Consideration must be given to the legal position of the forces, selection of *Rules of Engagement*, and the use of civil transport such as *Ships Taken Up From Trade (STUFT)*. The routeing of forces must be carefully considered, whether the deployment is to be covert or overt, protection of the deploying forces by, for example, *convoying* as well as logistic support of the deploying force.

## Sea Control Operations

Wherever the freedom of action of the maritime force is challenged and, in particular, as it approaches the area of operations, there will be a requirement to establish levels of sea control that will be sufficient to ensure its protection and to enable subsequent operations. Without sea control, the ability of maritime forces to manoeuvre, concentrate for offensive action, apply *leverage*, project power ashore, and deny the same to an opponent will be adversely constrained. As Chapter 4 explains, sea control is synonymous with dominance of the maritime portion of the battlespace. Influence over the battlespace allows the force's strengths to be used to advantage, while at the same time, protecting its combat power. The Carrier Task Group is the primary instrument of local sea control as well as a contributor to power projection. The nuclear powered attack submarine is a most potent *sea denial* system. The combination of a Carrier Task Group and such submarines creates a powerful and flexible force which together with other forces can adopt a variety of tactics to achieve sea control and execute power projection.

***Containment.*** Using their high transit speed, nuclear powered submarines can be despatched overtly ahead into theatre to pose a threat to enemy surface and submarine forces and valued land targets, and to tie down enemy forces in defence. Offensive minelaying might be used to enhance containment, if available and if *Rules of Engagement* (ROE) allow. If friendly shore based and *organic* attack aircraft from the carrier group are within range and the ROE allows, they might *interdict* port facilities, airfields and command and control installations and enemy surface shipping.

***Area and Barrier Operations.*** Submarines and maritime patrol aircraft conduct surveillance of the sea areas through which friendly naval surface forces and logistic shipping will in due course pass, locating and tracking submarine and surface targets and interdicting these as ROE allow. Helicopters from the carrier group might assist with prosecution of submarine and surface contacts when within range.

***Layered Defence.*** Before the naval task force enters waters where the threat is significant, the *Maritime Component Commander* will construct a layered defence about the force creating a moving area of robust sea control thereby protecting power projection forces and support. As the

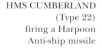

HMS CUMBERLAND
(Type 22)
firing a Harpoon
Anti-ship missile

force enters its operating areas off enemy territory, this area may become static. Layered defence consists of:

*Air Defence.* Organic *airborne early warning* (AEW) is provided by AEW aircraft from the carrier group. Fixed wing aircraft from the carrier group on *combat air patrol* provide the weapon systems for area air defence of the task force. Organic air defence aircraft would be integrated with shore based AWACS AEW aircraft and CAP when these are available. Shipborne area surface to air missiles supported by *electronic warfare* systems, radar and infra red systems provide the next layer of air defence against aircraft and missiles. Point defence missile systems can give protection to units close to the firing ship. Ultimately, surface ships use close in weapons systems (CIWS) and missile decoys for self defence.

*Anti-Submarine and Anti-Surface Defence.* Nuclear powered attack submarines and maritime patrol aircraft (MPA) in support of the force provide the outermost layer of anti-submarine and anti-surface defence. The next layer of anti-submarine defence is composed of frigates with long range sonar together with supporting MPA and organic helicopters, which will also assist in the location and prosecution of submarine contacts. The innermost layers of anti-submarine defence would be provided by helicopters using passive and active sonar and then surface ship hull mounted sonars. Helicopters from frigates and destroyers will act as weapon carriers and surface ships will use ship launched torpedoes and torpedo decoys for self defence. Shore based and organic fixed wing aircraft armed with air to surface missiles (ASM) can be tasked to interdict attacking surface ships. Helicopters with ASM will also provide anti-surface protection supplemented by ships' surface to surface missile systems.

*Precursor (Advance Sea Control) Operations.* During the transit phase an advance sea control group may be despatched to complement anti-submarine and anti-surface static area operations. These forces may also be used to establish elements of sea control[1] in any *holding areas* to be used by power projection forces as they poise offshore. Before an amphibious operation it may be necessary to conduct prolonged littoral sea control operations to eliminate any threat from fast attack craft and to reduce the risk from mines and conventional submarines to an acceptable level. During these operations mine countermeasures vessels are vulnerable to enemy attack and will need the protection of the force's defence umbrella. In preparation for an amphibious landing *advance operations* may involve the submarine insertion of special forces for *reconnaissance* and perhaps interdiction and the landing of beach control parties and *naval gunfire support* observers.

***Sea Lines of Support.*** Sea control operations must provide for the protection of reinforcement and resupply shipping not only to the naval task force but to the whole national intervention force. Once the naval task force is on station, this protection may require a separate operation involving the *escort* or *screening* of important units and, perhaps, full convoying.

***Afloat Support.*** Forces engaged in sea control operations will need afloat support which will either benefit from the wider sea control regime or will require its own layered defence. This support need not necessarily be independent of that provided to power projection operations. The replenishment of forces that are operating in outer layers of defence or on area operations needs careful planning as time off task while in transit and during replenishment must be minimized for both combat units and auxiliaries. For operations of long duration organic afloat support must be *consolidated*. The routes for consolidation shipping constitute campaign *lines of support*, and the ability to use them must be safeguarded.

## Power Projection Operations

With the establishment of appropriate levels of sea control, maritime forces are able to project power ashore. Power projection can take a number of forms; *amphibious operations*, naval air support, and surface and sub-surface land attack. A robust command and control system that, in the case of amphibious operations is capable of moving ashore, intelligence, concentration of combat power, and influence over the battlespace are critical functions for power projection operations. Co-ordination or even *synchronization* with land and air forces may be required.

*Amphibious Operations.* The Amphibious Task Group (ATG) projects amphibious power ashore, normally operating in conjunction with a Carrier Task Group. Types of amphibious operation that may form part of an intervention are discussed in Chapter 5. The full campaign may include operations to secure initial *access* to territory, manoeuvre from the sea, raids, feints, demonstrations, withdrawal and redeployment of the Landing Force, adjacent operations and subsidiary landings. Amphibious operations are arguably the most complex of all military operations,

RFAs Sir PERCIVALE
(LSL) and
Sir TRISTRAM (LSL)
off loading

co-ordinating as they do, many units at the juncture of all the operating environments. All amphibious operations will consist of a number of separate activities, some of which will run concurrently. These include:

- planning to establish the most suitable time and place to conduct the operation;
- *advance force operations* to gain intelligence, survey potential landing sites, deceive the enemy and disrupt his activities;
- establishment of the *amphibious objective area (AOA)* including, if necessary, mine countermeasures operations;
- the landing designed to establish the necessary combat power, logistic support and command and control capability ashore to carry out the task;
- and subsequent operations such as withdrawal for other tasks, the maintenance of a *lodgement area* to allow the introduction of follow-on forces, or military operations as part of a land campaign.

***Naval Air Support.*** Aircraft from the Carrier Task Group will contribute air defence of the battlespace *(counter air)*, *anti-surface force*, and *combat support* air operations in association with land based aircraft when available. Once *Joint Force Air Component Commander's (JFACC)* HQ is established in theatre, naval aircraft should be integrated into *joint* air forces. Air launched *land attack missiles* can complement *air interdiction* forces against a range of important targets.

***Surface and Sub-Surface Land Attack.*** Land attack missiles will also provide the primary means of organic long range attack in the early stages of a *conflict* and have particular utility for *coercion.* They will subsequently complement other air interdiction forces. Naval gunfire support will conduct advance bombardment and complement landing force artillery once this is landed. It is also available to other ground units operating in the littoral region.

## Sustainment of Operations

Once the focus of an intervention campaign moves ashore, the emphasis of maritime force operations will shift from being enabling to being supportive. That is not to say that the tasks assigned to maritime forces will alter, but the wider purpose to which those tasks will contribute will change. Although maritime forces will continue to provide intelligence and combat power in support of operations ashore, the principal operational functions during this stage are likely to be protection and logistic support: protection of units using the sea lines of support, of the maritime flank, and of logistic support to forces ashore and afloat, sustainment by *sealift*, and an alternative supply to *Host Nation Support (HNS)*.

## Withdrawal

The withdrawal of forces at the end of a successful campaign will require to be planned as carefully as the deployment to the area of operations. Indeed there may be the added complication of recovering unusable equipment,

Harriers operating from a CVSG

HMS SCEPTURE (SSN)
getting underway

and a political requirement for a speedy extraction and return. Moreover, if conditions for success have not been achieved, and withdrawal is to be made in the face of continuing or escalating conflict it will be even more problematical. There may be a need to increase combat power ashore to stabilize the situation before withdrawal can take place. Command and control will be difficult and fragmented (an afloat joint headquarters may provide secure and capable communications to markedly assist this function), and there will be a requirement to provide protection both for the maritime forces supporting withdrawal and for the forces being withdrawn. Protection of a withdrawal, like a landing but in reverse, requires the establishment of necessary levels of sea control.

## The Forces

*Nuclear Powered Ballistic Missile Submarines.* These deploy the missile systems to provide *strategic* and *sub-strategic nuclear deterrence* to the United Kingdom and to NATO. This function is more fully described in Chapters 2 and 5.

*Aircraft Carriers.* The Royal Navy's carriers (CVSG) are principal contributors to sea control, power projection and to the overall command and control of maritime operations. They operate a mixed air group consisting of *short take-off and vertical landing (STOVL)* jet fighter attack, reconnaissance and *close air support* aircraft, anti-submarine and AEW helicopters. The exact composition of the air group is tailored to the mission of the force. Organic air provides the ability to conduct independent air operations when it may not be possible to use bases ashore, coupled with the mobility to find clear flying conditions and rapid reactivity when the force is close to the combat zone. CVSGs provide essential command and control capabilities for a Naval Component Commander at the tactical level. At the operational level, when suitably augmented, they can provide a *Joint Force Headquarters* for a national *Joint Force Commander* or embark a NATO/WEU *Combined Joint Task Force* Commander. If required, a carrier can also be used to carry units of a Landing Force for operations of limited duration either as an LPH (see "Specialist Amphibious Shipping" below) or in the fast dash role. As an LPH it will only embark helicopters in support of land operations. In the *fast dash* role a tailored carrier air group (CAG) is embarked which could include fixed wing and AEW aircraft.

*Nuclear Powered Attack Submarines* are capable of high transit speeds and sustained underwater operations. They constitute a principal sea denial system having excellent

**2.** Commonly
referred to as Landing
Platform Dock (LPD)
and Landing Platform
Helicopter (LPH)

anti-submarine capabilities and an anti-ship capability using torpedoes and anti-surface missiles. When fitted with land attack missiles SSNs have a power projection capability of considerable range and penetrability with important uses for *naval diplomacy* (see Chapter 5). SSNs can gather intelligence and insert special forces. They can operate independently or in support of surface forces and contribute to the protection of the strategic nuclear deterrent.

## Amphibious Shipping

*Specialist Amphibious Shipping.* This comprises "Amphibious Transport, Docks" *(LPDs)*,[2] the "Amphibious Assault Ship, Helicopter" (LPH), if required a carrier in the amphibious role and Landing Ships Logistic (LSLs). In a potentially hostile environment they provide the transport and initial offload of the lead elements of a landing force in a tactical posture without recourse to harbours and airfields. They provide the launch platforms for assault landing by landing craft and support helicopter. LPDs have the necessary command and control facilities and are capable of landing heavy battle winning equipment, such as *armour*, as well as Commando vehicles and equipment. The LPH can accommodate a full Commando and deploy half the helicopters required for a 2 company group assault landing. *Landing Ships Logistic* (LSLs) provide *lift* for personnel and *materiel* additional to that provided by other specialist amphibious shipping. They also have helicopter spots, stern offload ramps and carry *Mexeflotes*, which are large, powered pontoons capable of offloading heavy stores and materiel from amphibious shipping and STUFT. Given satisfactory topography LSLs can also beach for rapid bow offload. They are fully integrated into any amphibious landing.

*Ship-to-Shore Movement Assets* comprise landing craft, Landing Craft Air Cushion (LCACs), Mexeflotes and support helicopters that are indigenous to the amphibious shipping. These assets can be transferred to the landing force on completion of a landing, thus providing it with tactical mobility in the absence of amphibious shipping. Helicopters enhance *tempo*, increase the Landing Force Commander's options, and in particular his ability to achieve depth in the initial phases of a landing, and the tactical flexibility of the force.

The other essential element of an amphibious capability is a Landing Force organised, trained and equipped for amphibious operations. This is provided primarily by 3 Commando Brigade Royal Marines and consists of three *Commandos*, a light artillery regiment (Royal Artillery), an air defence battery, a combat engineer squadron (Royal Engineers), a logistic regiment, a light helicopter squadron, a landing craft squadron, a headquarters and signal squadron with integral air defence, an EW capability, strategic communications and a long range patrol capability. The Brigade operates regularly with other Marine Corps, particularly with the Royal Netherlands Marine Corps (RNLMC) and United States Marine Corps. Under the terms of a Memorandum of Understanding the Brigade takes a RNLMC battalion group under command to form the UK Netherlands Amphibious Force (UKNLAF) for NATO and WEU operations. This example of effective binational cooperation is unique within NATO.

***Destroyers and Frigates.*** These are multi-purpose combatants with an emphasis on anti-air warfare or anti-submarine warfare but with capabilities in many disciplines. They are the smallest units that are deployed autonomously for military tasks and their numbers and capabilities allow them individually to cover a wide range of military, constabulary and benign tasks, particularly presence. They are also versatile building blocks for larger formations, essential defensive elements of task groups and contributors of organic helicopters to a force.

***Maritime Patrol Aircraft*** (MPA) The MPA's speed of transit, ability to cover large areas, and substantial capacity for weapons and recourse to shore supply makes it an

Hunt class MCM vessels

important contributor to anti-submarine and anti-surface warfare. They are particularly useful for area anti-submarine operations, surveillance and reconnaissance, if they can be based and supported within range of operations.

***Land based AEW, Air Defence and Attack Aircraft.*** These aircraft greatly improve the ability of maritime forces to operate in the face of enemy forces, if they can be based and supported within range and made available for maritime tasks.

***Mine Countermeasures Vessels (MCMV).*** MCMVs operate in support of the home base in critical waters. These include the approaches to friendly harbours and choke points where MCMVs are used to maintain the flow of shipping and access to the open ocean for nuclear powered ballistic missile firing submarines. In support of power projection, they are an important element of an amphibious force, particularly in precursor operations. They can also provide post-hostility mine clearance. MCMV will require a measure of forward support and a tasking authority if they are to be deployed for an extended period.

*Afloat Logistic Support* provides for the direct organic replenishment of fighting units and is required for any operation where a self-reliant naval force must be sustained at distance from shore bases. Ships of the *Royal Fleet Auxiliary* provide fuel, stores and ordnance while maintenance can be carried out by a Forward Maintenance and Repair Organization often deployed in a Forward Repair Ship (FRS). Many auxiliaries carry helicopters which can be integrated into the air assets of a formation. Specially equipped ships may be required to receive casualties if extensive combat is envisaged. Freighting support is required to move supplies from the main support area (usually the United Kingdom) to *Forward Logistics Sites* and to consolidate organic logistic shipping (see Chapter 8). Ships Taken up from Trade (STUFT) are used for this task and can be modified to carry helicopters.

*Ships Taken Up From Trade (STUFT).* The Amphibious Task Group will normally include STUFT to complement the lift provided by specialist amphibious shipping. STUFT may include transports for personnel (passenger vessels), vehicles *(RO-RO ferries)*, hospital ships, container ships, water ships, tankers and specialist lift shipping such as semi-submersibles to transport additional landing craft.

*Patrol Vessels.* Patrol craft are deployed around United Kingdom and her Dependent Territories' waters on constabulary tasks to protect offshore interests. They include units of the Fishery Protection and the Northern Ireland Squadrons. For fishery protection, the ships are under contract to the Ministry of Agriculture and Fisheries to patrol UK waters to protect UK fishing vessels and to enforce fisheries regulations. The Northern Ireland Squadron is the maritime contribution to counter-terrorism in that Province. The Ice Patrol Ship makes annual deployments to Antarctic waters to demonstrate British sovereignty interests, to provide assistance to the British

Antarctic Survey, and to undertake hydrographic survey and meteorological work.

*Hydrographic Vessels.* Survey vessels provide the surveying, charting, oceanographic and meteorological capability on which ships and submarines rely to navigate the seas safely and to exploit the environment to the full. They can also provide essential logistic and command support to MCMVs on distant deployment and during precursor operations, or act as Primary Casualty Receiving Ships (PCRSs). They can conduct tactical surveys in support of operations.

## People

People realise the level of capability that ships can provide. The United Kingdom has fully professional armed forces with a long history of excellence in leadership, training and motivation. These are world recognized strengths which we must continue to maintain, exploit and develop and which will require the allocation of adequate time, effort and resources.

### Life at Sea

Large numbers of sailors, marines, airmen, soldiers and, indeed, civilians live in very close proximity to each other for extended periods. The ship - their home for long periods in peace and conflict - is often uncomfortable. The maritime environment is featureless, tiring and demanding. Patterns of life during peacetime exercises differ little from those during hostilities. Maritime warfare is characterised by long periods of inactivity, surveillance and search followed by short bursts of intense combat. Concentration and alertness must not be allowed to drop during quieter periods. People, weapon systems and sensors must be welded together into a composite team.

*Leadership.* The relationship between command and leadership was described in Chapter 7. It is, however, not just the Commanding Officer who must be trained to lead. A ship's

HMS RICHMOND
(Type 23)

company is divided into departments, sub-departments and sections. At each level strong leadership will contribute to the effectiveness of the team and the smooth functioning of the ship. Leadership at all levels is a principal element in the maintenance of morale.

## Morale

The maintenance of good morale is a *Principle of War* (see Annex A). It is based on recognition of the needs of the individuals who collectively form the team and manifests itself in the will to win. Morale promotes the offensive spirit and determination to achieve the aim. Good morale is based on: a shared sense of purpose; clear understanding of and belief in, the aim; discipline and self-respect; confidence in equipment; training; and well-merited mutual trust and respect between those in and under command. The naval system of command and its long standing Divisional system provide a clear framework for effective leadership and support for the individual within the ship, or unit.

Supportive public opinion at home is also vital to the maintenance of morale, and the presentation by the media of the conduct of an operation and of the personalities involved assumes great significance. The ability of the operational commander to provide a clear, confident and credible message to those at home is crucial, but he must balance the need for security with that of accurate reporting from the operational area.

Operational success provides the quickest and most effective boost to morale for those at war but outstanding leadership will sustain high morale when all other factors are against it.

*Discipline.* Naval training instils discipline from the outset. Rather than being imposed from above, discipline rests within the individual. From self-discipline stems the spirit of teamwork and the willingness to be led.

## Training

The quality of the Royal Navy's training is respected world wide and is one of its greatest strengths. Training builds proficiency, cohesion and teamwork. It ranges from individual proficiency training to the conduct of large Task Force exercises which test command and control and the application of doctrine. Training enables operations to continue effectively in the confusion and stress of combat. The maintenance and demonstration of operational effectiveness through exercising is an essential part of the deterrent value of our armed forces.

Teamwork is essential within a ship if it is to be efficient and effective in combat. The requirement for good teamwork extends beyond the individual ship. It is also crucial within a force, where each unit must understand its contribution. If the task group has an international dimension the task of developing interoperability and forging corporate team spirit is equally important but more difficult to achieve. One of the basic building blocks is the establishment of standard tactical and operating procedures. Ships must continually hone their skills in these procedures to maximize their contribution to the force.

Realistic training maintains fleet operational effectiveness by preparing ships, task groups and task forces for war. Maritime task group and individual crew training can continue during passage to a theatre of operations thereby ensuring a high state of readiness on arrival. This may be invaluable for a multinational force whose individual units have little or no experience of operating together. Military training on passage is less easy to achieve, and the Landing Force and the individuals within it must be fully trained before deployment to theatre. A regular training pattern, including language training, wargaming, and *command post exercises (CPX)*, helps to reduce the need for pre-operational training.

## Conclusion

At first sight it might appear strange to link system capabilities and personnel matters in a single chapter but this is precisely the association that typifies combat at and from the sea. High technology equipment, complex command, control and information systems and highly trained and motivated personnel must function in complete harmony under conditions of stress and battle damage if maritime power is to be applied effectively. Individual vessels and aircraft are partners in the business of sea control and power projection whose capabilities must be meshed to bring success. Similar partnerships must exist between force, group and unit commanders, and, within each unit, between the people and the equipment they operate.

# Afterword

The Royal Navy and Royal Marines are accustomed to the mayhem of world events, but the Naval Service of today puts to sea in a particularly confused world in which security problems are not amenable to clear cut solutions. While the international problems of today may be eased, circumvented, or subject to compromise, they are rarely solved. Our predecessors experienced devastating violence and intense combat at first hand, but not perhaps equivalent complexities to today's global economics and communications, constraints of supranational authority and legality, challenges to traditional concepts of sovereignty and statehood, overabundance of information, and constant scrutiny by the press. In this environment positive forces must be united if there is to be progress. The Services must work closely together in the joint environment, and be adept at fusing our efforts with diplomatic and other channels of national power. British forces must not only be able to operate closely with Allies and friends, but must be seminal in enhancing the capability of multinational forces. Clarity of thought and expression is essential in this environment. Without it, planning will be diffuse and execution muddled. It is not a matter of dogmatic definitions and simple formulae for success, but of possessing the apparatus to understand how the military instrument can be used. The less structured the world and the more varied the challenges to security, the more vital the role doctrine plays in the deployment and employment of maritime forces. In guiding the actions of military forces in support of objectives, doctrine provides structure to chaos. Doctrine should give a common approach to warfighting based on a common understanding of the nature of war.

The preceding chapters have provided the reader with the fundamentals of British maritime doctrine, starting with its underpinning in the broader security and defence policies of the United Kingdom. They have examined the

183

general concepts of how a nation uses armed forces as instruments of policy, and then provided a comprehensive analysis of the nature of maritime power and how it is applied by the United Kingdom in the modern world. They have analyzed the vital factors of command and control and logistics and set out the basic principles of how an operation is planned. The reader, whatever his or her status or position should now have a much clearer idea of how the Royal Navy and the other components of British maritime power do their business.

Some aspects of doctrine are timeless; others reflect the best thinking and practice of the time. Although it is important that those concerned should be aware of contemporary terminology and concepts, they should not accept them slavishly. Indeed, the authors have tried to avoid making choices among options and laying down narrow dogmatic rules. They have endeavoured as far as possible to produce a guide to thinking, not a prescription for resulting thoughts.

This publication will be regularly revised to reflect current practice and thought. But doctrinal revision depends on the existence of a doctrine to revise. This book therefore sets out maritime doctrine as accepted at the date of publication. It should be treated with respect as an authoritative publication but not worshipped as holy writ. As we have seen, Nelson would not have done so, and neither should those who follow in his footsteps.

*Suggestions for improvement of this document should be forwarded to:-*

Maritime Doctrine Cell,
Maritime Warfare Centre,
HMS DRYAD,
Southwick,
Hampshire PO17 6EJ.

# The Principles of War

*Selection and Maintenance of the Aim.* In the conduct of all military operations it is essential to select and clearly define the aim. The ultimate aim is to break the will of the enemy to initiate war or to continue fighting once war has started. In war, each phase and each separate operation must be directed towards this supreme goal and all efforts must be directed to its attainment until a changed situation calls for a reappraisal and, consequently, a new aim. At any given time, a Commander should have only one aim. The aims of junior commanders must always contribute to that of their next superiors. Once decided this aim must be circulated as widely as security allows so that all can direct their efforts towards its achievement.

This Principle of War is the "Master Principle". The remaining principles are in no particular order, since their relative importance will vary according to the nature of the operation in question.

*Maintenance of Morale.* In the context of war, morale may be interpreted as the determination to achieve the aim. From this will spring courage, energy, skill and the bold offensive spirit. Good morale is based on a number of factors, including a shared sense of purpose, clear understanding of the aim, discipline and self respect, confidence in own equipment and a trust in the leadership. These days, public opinion and the effects of media coverage play an important part in the maintenance of morale.

*Offensive Action.* Offensive action is the chief means open to a commander to influence the outcome of a campaign or battle. It confers the initiative on the attacker, giving him the freedom of action necessary to secure a decision. Offensive action embodies a state of mind which is the determination to gain and hold the initiative: it is essential for the creation of confidence and to establish an ascendancy over

185

the enemy. It is closely allied to morale.

*Surprise.* Surprise is a most powerful influence in war, and its effect on morale is very great. Commanders at all levels must endeavour to surprise the enemy while safeguarding their own forces against surprise action. Surprise action can achieve results out of all proportion to the effort expended; indeed in some operations where other factors are unfavourable, surprise may be essential to success. Surprise can be achieved strategically, operationally, tactically or by the use of new weapons or material. The elements of surprise are secrecy, concealment, deception, originality, audacity and speed.

*Security.* A degree of security against enemy action is essential to all military operations. Security does not imply undue caution and avoidance of all risks, for bold action is essential to success. War is essentially a matter of taking calculated risks; the principle of security demands that these should be foreseen and either accepted or guarded against. It is not a breach of security to take risks but it is a serious breach not to realize they are being taken.

*Concentration of Force.* To achieve success in war it is essential to concentrate superior force against the enemy at the decisive time and place. Concentration may not mean the massing of forces in one place, but rather their deployment to enable the decisive blow to be delivered when and where required. Concentration of sufficient force to achieve the decisive task is perhaps the cardinal principle in the employment of armed forces in war. It may be said that the art of war is to decide the aim, then decide the tasks needed to achieve that aim, and then to concentrate the required forces into those tasks until the aim is achieved.

*Economy of Effort.* Economy of effort implies a balanced employment of forces and a judicious expenditure of the resources available to achieve the aim. If decisive strength is to be concentrated at the decisive time and place there must be no wasteful expenditure of effort where it cannot significantly affect the issue.

*Flexibility.* Conflict demands a high degree of flexibility to enable pre-arranged plans to be altered to meet changing situations and unexpected developments. This entails good training, organisation, discipline and staff work and, above all, that flexibility of mind and rapidity of decision on the part of both the Commander and his subordinates which ensures that time is never lost. It calls also for physical mobility so that forces can be concentrated rapidly and economically at the decisive time and place. Flexibility is therefore the capacity to cope with a rapidly changing situation and seize fleeting opportunities. It is inherent in maritime warfare and the mobility of maritime forces is their most valuable attribute.

*Cooperation.* Co-operation is based on team spirit and requires the co-ordination of all units to achieve the maximum combined effort from the whole. Co-operation between two forces or units often makes it possible to achieve something which neither could achieve separately. Above all, goodwill and a desire to co-operate are essential at all levels, not only within one Service, but also between the separate national Services and between allies.

*Administration.* Sound administration is a prerequisite for the success of any operation. Logistic considerations are often the deciding factor in assessing the feasibility of an operation. A clear appreciation of logistic constraints is as important to a commander as his ability to make a sound estimate of the operational situation. No plan can succeed without administrative support appropriate to the aim of the operation: it follows that a commander must have a degree of control over the administrative plan proportionate to the degree of his responsibility for the operation. Scarce resources must be controlled at a high level. The administrative organization must be flexible enough to react to changes in the situation with the most economic use of the available resources.

# The Falklands War 1982 from the Viewpoint of Doctrine

In April 1982, Argentine forces invaded the Falkland Islands and South Georgia taking them by force in a gamble based in part on the United Kingdom's limited *deterrent* posture in the South Atlantic. By mid-June the islands had been returned to full British sovereignty. Maritime power was the key to the successful outcome, and this account will concentrate on the maritime aspects of the *joint campaign*, relating them to the fundamentals of maritime *doctrine*.

The *grand strategic objective* to re-establish political control of the Falklands set the context and subordinate objectives of the whole campaign. The prompt despatch of the task forces was a *military strategic* act of military *coercion* in support of diplomatic efforts to secure a withdrawal. It was intended to demonstrate that the United Kingdom was prepared to back up its demand for the island's return to British control by force if necessary. However, it became clear that, despite international disapproval, the Argentine leadership could not be persuaded by such means, and it was necessary to retake the islands by force. Thus the mission changed from one of coercion to military repossession as the *crisis* developed, and a clear military *aim* was selected and maintained. The versatile *maritime force* was able to make the transition from coercion in support of diplomacy to *combat* operations after reinforcement. With long *lines of support* and a campaign of uncertain duration *logistics* were inevitably a dominant concern of operational and tactical commanders. In the event sustained reach was admirably demonstrated.

An early strategic and operational task was the establishment of suitable command and control arrangements. The British War Cabinet gave grand strategic direction and military strategic command was exercised from the Ministry of Defence in London. *Operational command* was vested in the Commander-in-Chief Fleet (CINCFLEET) at the designated

*Joint Headquarters* in Northwood, Middlesex. No single operational command was created in theatre. CINCFLEET commanded the two Naval Task Forces, the carrier and amphibious forces (TF317) and the nuclear powered submarines (TF324). The Land Force Commander, once established, also reported directly to the Joint Headquarters. However, before and during the landing the Commander Task Group 317.8, afloat in the carrier group, bore much operational as well as tactical responsibility. Once the amphibious lodgement was secure, command of land forces was transferred from the Commander Amphibious Forces afloat to the Land Forces Headquarters ashore. The command system proved to be less than perfect and caused a change to the current system, through the formal introduction of the Joint Commander and Joint Force Commander, described in Chapter 7.

On the Argentine side distinctions between levels of command were not clear cut. With a military junta that included heads of services in political as well as military power, grand strategic and military strategic levels were fused. An operational level could be said to have existed in the Argentinian Chiefs of Staff Committee where joint issues were addressed. Tactical command and control was complicated. Two commanders, the Air Force Commander on the mainland and the Military Governor at his Headquarters in Port Stanley, had simultaneous and common (but not joint) responsibility for the defence of the islands.

Care had to be taken with planning: few campaigns are fought in circumstances that are ideal for one side, but in this case, the difficulties were greater than normally considered acceptable for an attacking force:

- long lines of support lengthened the time taken for men and *materiel* to reach the theatre. Logistic feasibility limited the force which could be applied;

- the large Argentine garrison had had sufficient time to prepare defences;

- it was only in *naval forces* that there was a degree of parity, or even superiority: the Argentinians had overwhelming numerical superiority in the air, and a large numerical advantage on the ground;

- British forces faced combined pressures in maintaining offensive forces at high level far from shore support. They had to contend with wear and tear on ships, aircraft and weapons; the difficulties of keeping sailors and the embarked military force at acceptable degrees of training and *readiness* at sea over extended periods; the rigours of an approaching sub-Antarctic winter; and the apprehension that public support might not be infinitely sustainable. Furthermore, *Host Nation Support* was not available close to the operational area to ameliorate these problems.

- and despite international diplomatic support and contrary to policy extant for some 16 years this major amphibious operation was a purely national campaign.

Urgent planning was therefore essential to construct a campaign that would achieve its aim before British forces might reach their *culminating point* and be forced to withdraw. It was necessary to identify the *military conditions* that would bring about repossession of the islands and these were assessed as occupation of the centre of government at Stanley. The campaign was planned with this *end-state* in mind.

The protection of Task Force 317 and its main components was critical throughout, but the inherent *versatility*, *mobility* and *sustainability* of maritime forces provided a spectrum of offensive and defensive options. The task of taking Port Stanley could be approached in a number of ways. A direct assault against prepared defences where the bulk of Argentine ground forces were concentrated might shorten the campaign but would risk military disaster, particularly while the Argentines were still strong in the air and posed a naval threat. Preparations for the landing, by air and sea bombardment would alert the enemy and, besides, risk high casualties among the civilian population which the operation intended to set free.

The campaign plan was conceived to take advantage of maritime strengths while minimizing the more obvious military risks. *Attrition* on the Argentine navy and air force to weaken the off-island defensive capability, if it could not be neutralized, would be followed by an *amphibious assault*, and then by an investment of Port Stanley. In the event the landing was conducted in a remote area and followed by an overland advance on the defences of the capital.

The British campaign was *sequential* and had six phases. First, nuclear powered attack submarines were deployed early into the theatre, exploiting their characteristics of speed and stealth, to collect intelligence and to begin *surveillance* of the Argentine naval forces. They established a *military exclusion zone* around the islands designed to support coercive diplomacy and prevent reinforcement.

Meanwhile the second phase consisting of the assembly of the main task force, its deployment and use for coercion was underway. Here, shore support was crucial. Assembly involved the gathering of ships from several ports both at home and abroad, storing and general preparation for *war*. Urgent procurement programmes were set up with the help of industry to produce some items of specialist equipment. Afloat support in a distant area over an indefinite period would require not only the ships of the Royal Fleet Auxiliary with the task force but also a large number of civilian vessels to provide second echelon support (Ships Taken Up From Trade) to achieve sustained reach.

It was decided to mount an operation using a portion of the Task Group to retake South Georgia (Phase 3). This would not only dispose of any potential the enemy had for outflanking the British forces but, if successful, would transmit intent to the Argentines and buoy up British spirits. By now, the Task Group was well on its way south. Ascension Island was set up as an *advanced logistic support site*, being used both as an airhead and STUFT tanker base in support of the Joint Operational Logistics Pipeline. An advanced force was detached with Royal Marine and Special Forces to retake South Georgia. After some difficulties, this was achieved on 25 April; the capture of one of the enemy's three serviceable submarines was a bonus.

The fourth phase required the establishment of a *blockade* around the Falkland Islands to prevent reinforcement, and measures to achieve a sufficient degree of *sea control* to permit a landing. A *total exclusion zone* was declared but in the event there were not enough *counter-air* forces to prevent continual Argentinian resupply of the Islands by air.

On 2 May, the British nuclear powered submarine HMS CONQUEROR sank the Argentine cruiser GENERAL BELGRANO. This resulted in the *containment* of the remaining Argentine surface forces, including a carrier, which played no further part in the campaign, thereby reducing a major challenge to British sea control. However, the loss of HMS SHEFFIELD to missile attack demonstrated the powerful *sea denial* capabilities still possessed by Argentine maritime air forces. Furthermore the remaining Argentine submarines posed a residual threat as a *fleet in being* and it was necessary to continue to devote much time and effort to anti-submarine protection.

During the first three weeks of May, a series of offensive operations was conducted with the following objectives:

**Attrition.** A *cumulative* operation to stimulate action with Argentine air forces, preferably on terms unfavourable to them to reduce their initial superiority, through air combat and Destroyer/Frigate missile traps.

**Sea Denial.** A blockade to stop or hinder the reinforcement and resupply of the Argentine garrison on the Islands by fixed and rotary-wing air attacks, sweeps by Surface Action Groups and implicit threat of submarine action.

**Advance Force Operations.** Operations in advance of landing main ground forces by submarine, air and clandestine reconnaissance, suppression of defences and radars, and air-raids to demoralize the garrison.

**Deception.** Diversionary operations (bombardments, *raids* and other activities) intended to mislead the enemy's interpretation of British intentions and to *distract* defending forces.

This influence over the battlespace created the conditions necessary for *maritime power projection*, and enabled the landing of a force at a place which combined operational attractiveness with a degree of insurance against enemy retaliation before the troops could become established. Never exposing any critical vulnerability to undue risk, these activities also maintained the initiative, sustained the *tempo* of the campaign, and raised morale within the Task Force as a whole.

On 20 May the fifth phase began with a full-scale assault in San Carlos Water, an inlet off the Falkland Sound. It was chosen to make the task for the Argentine land and air forces as difficult as possible by exploiting the capacity of maritime forces to achieve surprise and concentration of force. This used all the available amphibious units supported by various warships and auxiliaries, whilst the aircraft carriers stood off, supplying *counter-air* and *offensive air support*. Air superiority over the *amphibious objective* area could not be guaranteed but a *favourable air situation* was exploited during darkness when the enemy aircraft did not fly. It was during the subsequent build-up phase that the desired attrition rates of Argentine aircraft were finally achieved, although at a cost of warships lost and put out of action. Although the Argentines eventually realized that the landings were the main effort, not a diversion, their lack of response had allowed sufficient build-up of combat power to ensure the security of the British lodgement.

Once the breakout (Phase 6) had begun, the land forces advanced steadily against the main Argentine positions, with direct and logistic support supplied by the naval Task

Group. Major setbacks, such as the sinking of the ATLAN-TIC CONVEYOR with her cargo-carrying helicopters and irreplaceable stores, dictated substantial alterations to the offensive plan for advance, demonstrating the vulnerability caused by long lines of support. Nevertheless, momentum was maintained by prioritization, improvisation and the flexibility of maritime support. Outnumbering the attacking troops but harried by air attack (now from forward operating bases), air portable artillery and *naval gunfire support*, Argentinian troops were in the space of a few days driven by pressure of *manoeuvre*, the tempo and *simultaneity* of operations, and head-on assault from their strong defensive positions. A final seventh phase, the investment of Port Stanley, was beginning when on 14 June 1982, the ill-supplied and demoralized garrison, reduced to military disorder, surrendered at Port Stanley. The military *conditions for success* were met. The following morning the Governor's flag was again hoisted after an absence of 74 days - the United Kingdom's *war aim*, its *grand strategic objective*, had been achieved.

# Glossary

*The references quoted in brackets after some entries are source documents.*

## Source Documents

| | |
|---|---|
| **AAP6** | NATO Glossary of Terms and Definitions |
| **ADP Vol 1** | Army Doctrine Publication Volume 1: Operations |
| **AFM WP** | Army Field Manual: Wider Peacekeeping |
| **AJP1(A)** | Allied Joint Operations Doctrine |
| **AP3000** | Royal Air Force Air Power Doctrine - 2nd Edition |
| **FM100-5** | Field Manual 100-5: Operations (United States Army)) |
| **JSP1** | Joint Service Doctrine |
| **JSP110** | Joint Service Glossary |
| **NDP1** | Naval Doctrine Publication 1: Naval Warfare (United States Navy) |
| **OED** | Concise Oxford English Dictionary |
| **SDE** | Statement of Defence Estimates (Annual) |
| **STANAG 1166** | Standard Ship Designator System |

# A

*Access (Military)* The freedom of action to manoeuvre to achieve control of a designated environment or to bring target sets within range of organic firepower or other military capabilities.

*Administration* The management and execution of all military matters not included in tactics, [operations] and strategy; primarily in the fields of logistics and personnel management. (JSP 110)

*Administrative authority* A commander vested with those aspects of command that are concerned with administration. See *full command.*

*Advanced Logistic Support Site (ALSS)* The primary transhipment point for materiel and personnel destined to and from afloat units. In a NATO operation the ALSS commander reports to the *Multinational Logistic Commander (MNLC)*. Daily coordination must be conducted with *Forward Logistics Sites (FLS)*.

**Advance Force Operations** *Advance operations* to prepare an *amphibious objective area* for the main assault by conducting such operations as *reconnaissance*, seizure of supporting positions, precursor mine countermeasures operations, preliminary bombardment (by *naval gunfire support*), underwater demolitions and air support. (from JSP110)

**Advance operation** Operation in advance of a main force. Advance operations include *precursor* operations and *advance force operations*.

**Aim (Military)** A single unambiguous military purpose that must be established before a plan can be developed at any level of command and planning for armed conflict (*level of war*). A *mission* or directive may spawn a number of military *objectives*. Part of mission analysis is to resolve these objectives into a single aim and subordinate objectives.

**Airborne early warning (AEW)** Air surveillance and control provided by airborne vehicles equipped with radar and communications equipment for controlling weapon systems. (AP 3000)

**Air interdiction (AI)** An air operation conducted to destroy, disrupt, neutralize or delay the enemy's military potential before it can be brought to bear effectively against friendly forces. (AP 3000)

**Air superiority** That degree of dominance in the air battle of one force over another which permits the conduct of operations by the former and its related land, sea and air forces at a given time and place without prohibitive interference by the opposing force. (AP 3000)

**Air supremacy** That degree of air superiority wherein the opposing air force is incapable of effective interference. (AP 3000)

*Amphibious assault* The principal type of amphibious operation involving establishment of a force on a hostile or
potentially hostile shore. [AJP1(A)]

*Amphibious demonstration* An amphibious operation conducted to *deceive* an enemy in order to make him take up
positions which are unfavourable to him [AJP1(A)].

*Amphibious feint* A ruse with the purpose of *distracting* the
action of an enemy force by posing an amphibious threat to
be countered.

*Amphibious group* *Task group* or *battlegroup* whose core is an
amphibious command ship and amphibious shipping and a
landing force and whose purpose is principally to deliver
amphibious capability.

*Amphibious objective area (AOA)* A geographical area, delineated in the initiating *directive*, for purposes of *command and
control* within which is located the objective(s) to be secured
by the amphibious task force. This area must be of sufficient
size to ensure accomplishment of the amphibious task
force's mission and must provide sufficient area for conducting necessary sea, land and air operations. [AJP1(A)]

*Amphibious operation* An operation launched from the sea
onto the land by naval and landing forces.

*Amphibious raid* A type of amphibious operation involving
the swift incursion into or temporary occupation of an
objective followed by a planned withdrawal. (JSP 110)

*Amphibious withdrawal* A type of operation involving the
extraction of force by sea in naval ships or craft from a
hostile or potentially hostile shore. [AJP1(A)]

*Anti-surface force air operations* Operations to deprive the
enemy of the military power he needs to occupy territory or
exploit seaspace. They involve the use of airpower in co-
operation with friendly surface and sub-surface forces to
*deter, contain* or defeat the enemy's army and/or
navy.(AP3000)

*Appreciation* See *Commander's Appreciation of the Situation.*

*Archipelagic waters* Waters over which an *Archipelagic State* claims increased sovereignty under the United Nations Convention on Law of the Sea 1982 (UNCLOS 82). The United Kingdom Government's view is that the relevant articles of UNCLOS 82 are far from satisfactory. It therefore considers each archipelagic claim individually.

*Archipelagic State* An independent state consisting entirely of an archipelago of islands.

*Area Forces* Maritime forces declared to NATO at similar levels of readiness to the force categories of *Reaction* and *Main Defence Forces,* but not allocated to *Multinational NATO Maritime Forces.*

*Area of influence* A geographical area wherein a commander is directly capable of influencing operations, by *manoeuvre* or fire support systems normally under his command and control. [AJP1(A)]

*Area of interest* The area of concern to the commander, including *area of influence,* areas adjacent thereto, and extending into enemy territory to the objectives of current or planned operations. This area also includes areas occupied by enemy forces who could jeopardize the accomplishment of the mission.[AJP1(A)]

*Armed suasion* The use of military forces in support of diplomacy to influence the decisions of a government or quasi-governmental authority (such as the leadership of a faction). Suasion can be latent (as in *presence* and general *deterrence*) or active. Active suasion can be supportive (as in *coalition building*) or *coercive* in which case it can seek to *deter* or *compel.*

*Armour* Tanks and armoured reconnaissance vehicles.

*Assault* See *Amphibious assault.*

*Attrition* The reduction of the effectiveness of a force caused by loss of personnel and material. (JSP 110)

*Attrition warfare* A style of warfare characterized by the application of overwhelming combat power that reduces an enemy's ability to fight through loss of personnel and equipment. Contrasted with *manoeuvre warfare* in a debate that began during the First World War and has continued into the latter part of the 20th Century.

*Augmentation Forces (AF)* Constitute the balance of forces declared to NATO, in addition to *Reaction Forces* and *Main Defence Forces*, necessary for full scale conflict. They can be maintained at longer readiness and are structured primarily to fulfil the remaining tasks of reinforcement and defence of NATO territory.

*Auxiliary* A vessel other than a warship operated by the Royal Navy for logistic and other purposes and usually manned by civilian personnel. The two Auxiliary Services are the Royal Fleet Auxiliary and the Royal Maritime Auxiliary Service.

# B

*Balanced force* A military force that has all the necessary capabilities to carry out a particular *mission* without unnecessary redundancy.

*Balanced fleet* Colloquial expression for a naval force that can be generated and sustained with a full range of capabilities for such independent (unilateral) strategic and operational action as is envisaged in defence policy and national military strategy.

*Balance of advantage* The qualitative advantage of a force over an opposing force taking into account quantity, quality and categories of capability. See *exchange ratio*.

*Battlefield air interdiction (BAI)* Air action against hostile land targets which are in a position to affect friendly forces directly but not in contact. BAI requires *joint* planning and co-ordination. (AP 3000)

***Battleforce*** A force comprising several *battlegroups*. A battleforce is typically a three star command and equates in NATO Reaction Force parlance to a *NATO Expanded Task Force*.

***Battlegroup*** A functional formation comprising major vessels and screening units, for instance a *Carrier Group* or an *Amphibious Group*. A battlegroup is typically a one or two star command.

***Battlespace*** All aspects of air, surface, subsurface, land, space and the electromagnetic spectrum that encompass the area of operations, *area of influence* and *area of interest* in a *campaign* or operation. (US NDP1)

***Battlespace, influence over the*** See *influence over the battlespace*.

***Battlespace dominance*** The degree of control over the dimensions of the *battlespace* that enhances friendly freedom of action and denies the enemy freedom of action. It permits *power projection* and force sustainment to accomplish the full range of potential missions. (US NDP1)

***Beachhead*** Designated area on a hostile shore which, when seized and held, ensures the continuous landing of troops and material, and provides *manoeuvre* space requisite for subsequent projected operations ashore. (JSP110)

***Benign application (or use) of force*** The use of armed forces solely for the capabilities not directly associated with combat that they can provide. Blockade A legal definition is "An operation intended to disrupt the enemy's economy by preventing ships of all nations from entering or leaving specified coastal areas under the occupation and control of the enemy. Blockade is an act of war and the right to establish it is granted to belligerents under the traditional laws of war. This law requires, inter alia, that the blockade must be effective, that it is to be declared by the belligerent so that all interested parties know of its existence and that it is confined to ports or coasts occupied by the enemy." The expression is used more broadly to mean a *combat* operation carried out to prevent access to, or departure from the coast or waters of a hostile state.

**Blue on blue engagement** (colloquial) Accidental combat between own, allied or friendly forces.

**Branch** (in operational planning) A contingency plan or option built into a plan for changing the disposition orientation, or direction of movement of forces, and also for accepting or declining battle (US FM100-5). A form of "what if?".

# C

**Campaign** A sequence of planned, resourced and executed military *operations* designed to achieve a strategic *objective* within a given time and area, usually involving the *synchronization* of maritime, land and air forces [AJP1(A)]. Campaigns may be *sequential* or *cumulative*. The orchestration of campaigns is the business of the *operational commander*.

**Cantonment** Custody by *peacekeeping* forces of the vessels or other forces of one or more of the erstwhile belligerent parties.

**Carrier Group** *Task group* or *battlegroup* whose core is a carrier and whose function is principally to deliver carrier capabilities.

**Catastrophic damage** The sudden loss of a substantial collection of resources and capabilities, such as the sinking of a major warship.

**Centre of gravity** Those characteristics, capabilities, or localities from which enemy [and friendly forces] derive their freedom of action, physical strength or will to fight [AJP1(A)]. The expression is derived from Clausewitz' work On War. It is used at the strategic and operational levels but not at the tactical level.

***Civil war*** War conducted largely within the boundaries of a state in which a significant part of the population is associated with each side and in which the contest is for the government of the state or for autonomy for or secession of one or more regions.

***Close air support (CAS)*** Air action against hostile targets which are in close proximity to friendly forces and which require detailed integration of each air mission with the fire and movement of those forces. (AP 3000)

***Close blockade*** A *blockade* that denies an enemy access to or from his ports. See *distant blockade*.

***Close escort*** *Escort* of shipping where the escorting force is in company with escorted shipping and can provide a measure of direct defence.

***Close operations*** Land operations which involve friendly forces in direct contact with the enemy. They are usually conducted at short range and in an immediate timescale. (ADP Vol 1)

***Coalition building*** Military action in support of diplomacy to further the building of an ad hoc coalition by providing reassurance, evidence of support and, perhaps, the opportunity for military meetings in theatre.

***Coercion*** Military coercion is the use of armed forces to achieve objectives by the direct effect of their posture or actions on the decision making process of an opponent rather than by destruction of his military capability. Outside hostilities *coercion* may be used in support of diplomacy to persuade an opponent to desist from a course of action (*compellance*) or to dissuade him from undertaking one (*deterrence*). Discrete acts of *combat* may be used to reinforce coercion.

***Collateral damage*** Destruction of or damage to property and equipment and personnel that is caused by *combat* but incidental to its purpose.

*Combat* Military combat is a contest in which the parties attempt to achieve mutually incompatible aims through the organized use of *violence* by armed forces.

*Combat air patrol (CAP)* Patrols by fighter aircraft over an objective area, a force to be protected, over the critical area of a combat zone or over an air defence area for the purpose of intercepting and destroying hostile aircraft before they reach their targets. (AP 3000)

*Combat governed application (or use) of force* See the *military application of force.*

*Combat Power* One of the *operational functions.* Combat power is the product of the combat systems in a force and the ability to bring the firepower generated by these systems to bear effectively.

*Combat service support (CSS)* A term used principally in land operations for those essential logistic functions, activities and tasks necessary to sustain soldiers and their weapon systems in an area of operations.

*Combat support air operations* Air operations designed to enhance or support the effectiveness of air, surface and sub-surface combat forces.(AP3000)

*Combined* Between two or more forces or agencies of two or more allies [AJP1(A)]. The expressions "combined forces" and "combined operations" imply that the command and control of allied forces is integrated. See *coordination; concertation; integration;* and *multinational.*

*Combined Joint Task Force (CJTF)* A multinational multi-service task force. The CJTF Headquarters Concept provides for deployable multinational multi-service headquarters of variable size formed to command and control CJTFs of NATO and possibly non-NATO nations. A CJTF HQ could also be deployed for WEU led operations.

*Command* The authority vested in an individual of the Armed Forces for the direction, coordination and control of military forces [AJP1(A))]. See *full command.*

***Command and Control*** (C2) Expression used to mean:
1. The processes through which a *commander exercises command (whether full or Operational or Tactical Command)* or *Operational or Tactical Control* to organize, direct and coordinate the activities of the forces allocated to him.
2. The structures and systems through which these processes are exercised. A command, control,[communications] and information system (C3I) is an integrated system comprising *doctrine*, procedures, organizational structure, personnel, equipment, facilities, and communications, which provides authorities at all levels with timely and adequate data to plan, direct and control their activities [from AJP1(A)].

***Command and Control Warfare (C2W)*** The integrated use of physical destruction, electronic warfare, *psychological operations* and *operational security*, supported by intelligence, to deny information to, exploit, influence, degrade, confuse or destroy enemy command and control C2) capabilities and to protect friendly C2, against such actions. [AJP 1(A)]

***Commander Allied Joint Force (COMAJF)*** In NATO the commander appointed by a *MNC* or *MSC* to mount and sustain an Allied operation and to exercise OPCON of all the forces assigend to the operation. [AJP1(A)]

***Commander's Appreciation of the Situation*** The classical British expression for what has come to be known in combined and joint parlance as the *Commander's Estimate of the Situation.*

***Commander's Estimate of the Situation*** A formal analysis of the operational situation, mission, enemy and own courses of action conducted in preparation for forming a *commander's intentions* and *concept of operations.*

***Commander's Intentions*** A concise expression of the purpose of a *campaign* or *operation*, the desired results and how operations will progress towards these results.

***Commando*** A Royal Marine formation of battalion size with combat support and *combat service support.*

**Command of the sea** The ability to use the sea in its entirety for ones own purposes at any time and to deny the use of ships to the enemy.

**Compel/Compellance** The *coercive* use of armed forces to persuade a government by the threat or isolated use of combat to desist from a course of action.

**Component Commander** The commander of the maritime, ground, air, or other component of a *Joint Force* (UK national) or *Combined Joint Task Force* (NATO/WEU) and reporting to the *Joint Force Commander* or *Combined Joint Task Force Commander* respectively.

**Command post exercise (CPX)** An exercise in which the forces are simulated involving commanders, their staffs and communications within and between headquarters. (from JSP110)

**Concept of operations** A clear and concise statement of the line of action chosen by a commander in order to accomplish his mission. [AJP1(A)]

**Concerted multinational operations** (basic cooperation) Operations in which forces of more than one friendly or allied nation are operating in the same theatre but without formal arrangements to coordinate operations or an integrated command structure. They cooperate to the extent that mutual interference may be minimized, information may be exchanged and some logistic support and mutual training offered.

**Conditions for success** The situation and state of affairs that must pertain if a military campaign or operation can be considered successful. The conditions may be *military conditions* which are normally expressed as control of the environment, or may be non-military such as the decision of a hostile government to desist from action. See *end state*.

**Conflict** A situation in which violence becomes a possibility in the external relations between nations or violence is threatened or used within a state's borders between competing groups for political reasons beyond levels that might be controlled by levels of civilian policing that are normal for that state.

***Conflict prevention*** Activity designed to anticipate and forestall the development of conflict using diplomatic, economic and, on occasion, military means. Military means include the establishment of early warning arrangements, *surveillance*, stabilizing measures and *preventive deployment*.

***Consolidation*** The replenishment of organic *logistic* shipping by freighting vessels.

***Constabulary application (or use) of force*** The use of military forces to uphold a national or international law, mandate or regime in a manner in which minimum violence is only used in enforcement as a last resort and after evidence of a breach or intent to defy has been established beyond reasonable doubt. The level and type of violence that is permitted will frequently be specified in the law, mandate or regime that is being enforced. Also called policing.

***Containment***
1. Military containment The geographical restriction of the freedom of action of enemy forces.
2. Crisis containment Measures to limit the geographical spread of a crisis.
3. Containment as grand strategy Measures taken to limit the geographic spread of an ideology or the influence of a power.

***Containment by Distraction*** Containment achieved by posing so great a threat to an enemy in one area (particularly in home waters or close to critical interests) that enemy forces are retained in defence allowing friendly forces elsewhere to be unmolested.

***Contingency forces*** Forces required to undertake *Military Tasks* across all three UK *Defence Roles* other than: first, those forces permanently stationed at home and abroad; and, secondly, those additional forces that would be *regenerated* and/or *reconstituted* in the event of general war.

***Control***
1. That authority exercised by a commander over part of the activities of subordinate organizations, or other organizations not normally under his command, which encompasses the responsibility for implementing orders or directions. All or part of this authority may be transferred or delegated. (JSP 110)
2. The process through which the commander organizes, directs and coordinates the activities of the forces allocated to him.
3. Military control (of the environment) is the condition in which one protagonist has freedom of action to use one or more *warfare environments* (land, sea, air, space or electromagnetic spectrum) for his purposes and to deny its use to an opponent. See *sea control; control of the air.*

***Control of the air*** The three degrees of control of the air are: *favourable air situation; air superiority;* and *air supremacy.* (AP 3000)

***Convoying*** The aggregation of shipping to be protected into groups to reduce losses through enemy action, to make best use of protective forces and to increase losses of enemy attacking forces.

***Co-operation, multinational operations under basic*** See *concerted multinational operations.*

***Co-ordinated multinational operations*** Operations in which participating friendly or allied nations share objectives to the extent that formal arrangements can be made to apportion tasks or areas of responsibility and to provide mutual assistance. However there is no integrated command structure.

***Counter-air operations*** Operations to achieve and maintain the required degree of *control of the air.*

***Counter-insurgency operations*** Military operations carried out to complement those political, economic, psychological and civic actions necessary to defeat an armed *insurgency* and thereby sustain an existing government's authority. (ADP Vol 1)

***Counter-terrorism*** Measures taken to prevent, deter, and respond to terrorism. (US FM 100-5) Crisis A situation that threatens national objectives, interrupts the normal process of government, and/or creates an expectation of hostilities and hence a sense of urgency. After the onset of regular combat a worsening of levels of violence is more appropriately termed *escalation*.

***Crisis management*** Measures taken to modify a *crisis*. They include *crisis prevention* and crisis control. Crisis control consists of measures to *contain* and to reduce a crisis.

***Crisis prevention*** Diplomatic and economic and, on occasion, military measures to modify the causes of a potential crisis and prevent its onset.

***Critical vulnerability*** A vulnerability in a force's fighting system which, if destroyed or otherwise controlled, will lead to *systemic disruption* of that force.

***Culminating point/Culmination*** The point in time and place when the attacker's *combat power* no longer exceeds that of the defender. The defender reaches culmination when he no longer has the capacity to defend successfully or mount a counter-offensive.

***Cumulative campaign*** A campaign the outcome of which is the result of the cumulative effect of a number of independent actions. See *sequential campaign*.

***Deception*** Those measures designed to mislead by manipulation, distortion, or falsification of evidence to induce an opponent to react in a manner prejudicial to his interests. (JSP 110)

# D

***Decisive event*** A military event such as a battle or encounter that creates a decision that defines the course of subsequent events. In a plan that seeks to keep the initiative a commander will attempt to identify and bring about decisive events on his terms. When the commander can identify decisive events, he should concentrate force to achieve them.

***Decisive point*** An intermediate objective the prosecution of which will provide a marked advantage. Decisive points are frequently geographic locations to be seized but may be characteristics or capabilities of the enemy. They may be multiple and are distinct from the *centre of gravity*. However, they may provide an avenue to the centre of gravity.

***Deep operations*** Land operations conducted at long range and over a protracted timescale against the enemy's forces or resources not currently engaged in the *close* battle. They expand the battlefield in time and space making it difficult for the enemy to concentrate combat power without loss, and thus diminish the coherence and *tempo* of his actions. (ADP Vol 1)

***De-escalation*** A decrease in the level or extent of *violence* during *hostilities*. See *escalation*.

***Defence in depth*** Operational concept to achieve a sufficient degree of sea control for protection of own forces by a combination of capabilities and proactive and reactive methods including area operations, barrier operations and *screens*. It is also a NATO Principle of Maritime Warfare.

***Defence Role (DR)*** One of three overlapping formal roles for the UK armed forces that were first published in *SDE* 92 and are used to express UK Defence Policy.

***Defensive operation*** Operation in which forces await for the approach of the enemy before attacking.

***Demarche*** Formal request or statement of policy or opinion issued through diplomatic channels by a government alliance, coalition or group of nations.

**Demobilization operations** In the context of *peace support operations*, the controlled withdrawal, demobilization and rehabilitation of belligerents (AFM WP). They might include *cantonment* of belligerents' vessels.

**Demonstration** (See *Amphibious demonstration*)

**Deterrence** A possible aggressor is deterred if he fails to act because he assesses that the cost of any aggressive action will outweigh any benefits. Deterrence is a form of *coercion*. It can be general when no specific aggressor or act of aggression is identified, or directed at a specific government to deter specific actions. Deterrence can be enacted through nuclear or conventional forces.

**Directive** A strategic directive is issued to the *operational commander* by the military strategic authority, which in the case of independent UK operations will be the Chief of the Defence Staff. It should contain the strategic *goals, conditions for success*, political constraints, financial limitations and available forces and resources. (ADP Vol 1)

**Dislocation** The denial to an enemy of the ability to bring his strengths to bear. (ADP Vol 1)

**Disruption** The shattering of the cohesion of a formation or combat system thereby preventing it from functioning effectively and therefore from performing successfully in combat. It may be achieved physically by destruction of elements essential for cohesion such as *command, control*, communications and information systems or *logistics*, or psychologically by affecting the decisions of the command and other individuals by surprise, *deception*, or the effects of *simultaneity*.

**Distant blockade** A *blockade* that denies the enemy passage through a sea area through which all ships must pass in order to reach the enemy's territory.

**Distant escort** *Escort* of shipping where the protective forces are not sufficiently close to provide a measure of direct defence but effect protection by *deterrence* through the threat of reprisals.

**Distraction** Situation in which an enemy is unable to concentrate forces in a time and place of his choosing because of the threat of attack elsewhere.

**Doctrine** Fundamental principles by which the military forces guide their actions in support of objectives. It is authoritative but requires judgement in application. (JSP 110)

# E

**Echelonment** The organization of formations at each level of command from lower level formations. Echelonment of maritime forces is very flexible and makes use of *functional* or *task organization.*

**Economy of force operation** A *distractive* or *defensive* operation using modest resources so as to concentrate force for the main effort. Sometimes called a *holding operation* when associated with an offensive manoeuvre.

**Élan** Offensive spirit. Ardour.

**Electronic warfare** Offensive and defensive exploitation of the electromagnetic spectrum for the purposes of *combat.*

**Embargo** A prohibition on the entry or egress of shipping into a port. Nowadays frequently used for prohibitions of certain categories of cargo such as munitions.

**Embroilment** Military embroilment is the involvement of forces in *conflict* at a level of *violence* that is greater than that for which they are equipped or prepared or that envisaged in their strategic *directive.*

**End-state** That state of affairs which needs to be achieved at the end of a campaign either to terminate or resolve the conflict on favourable terms.

**Endurance** The ability of a unit or formation to maintain an operational commitment for a protracted period. It is also used to mean the length of period that a unit or formations can maintain a commitment. See *sustainability*.

***Envelopment/envelop*** An offensive *manoeuvre* in which the main attacking force passes around or over the enemy's principal defensive position to secure objectives in the rear. (AAP 6)

***Escalation*** An increase in the level, extent or duration of *violence* during *hostilities*. See *vertical escalation, horizontal escalation, qualitative escalation* and *prolongation*.

***Escort***
1. A method of protection of shipping short of the establishment of full *sea control* in which protection is achieve primarily by the *deterrent* presence of protective forces.
2. Colloquial generic expression for a destroyer or frigate.

***Exchange ratio*** The numerical ratio of friendly to enemy forces taking into account quantity, quality and categories of capability. See *balance of advantage*.

***Exclusive Economic Zone (EEZ)*** The zone of sea around a state over which it has exclusive rights under international law to exploit economic resources.

***Expeditionary forces*** Forces projected from the home base capable of sustained operations at distance from that home base.

# F

***Fast dash role*** The use of a United Kingdom carrier in an amphibious role to carry elements of a landing force, and assault helicopters as the principal component of the carrier air group.

***Favourable air situation*** An air situation in which the extent of air effort applied by the enemy air forces is insufficient to prejudice the success of friendly land, sea or air operations. (AP 3000)

*Feint* (*see amphibious feint*)

*Fighting Instructions* Classified publication containing Royal Navy operational and tactical doctrine.

*Fleet in being* The use of options provided by the continued existence of one's own fleet to constrain the enemy's options in the use if his.

*Fog of war* Uncertainty and confusion generated in wartime by a combination of limited, incomplete, inaccurate and contradictory information, deliberate deception and the mayhem and stress caused by combat. From Clausewitz' On War.

*Forward line of own troops (FLOT)* A line which indicates the most forward positions of friendly forces in any kind of military operation at a specified time (JSP 110). Primarily used in land operations.

*Forward Logistics Site (FLS)* Normally the final land tranship-ment point for *materiel* and personnel which provides a bridge between an *Advanced Logistic Support Site (ALSS)* and the sea. It will be linked to the ALSS by intra-theatre airlift. In a NATO operation the FLS commander reports directly to the *Multinational Logistic Commander (MNLC)*. Daily coor-dination with the ALSS commander must be conducted.

*Forward presence* Strategic choice to maintain forces deployed at distance from the home base or stationed overseas to demonstrate national resolve, strengthen alliances, dissuade potential adversaries, and enhance the ability to respond quickly to contingencies.

*Fratricide* The accidental destruction of own, allied or friendly forces. A result of what is colloquially known as a *blue on blue engagement.*

*Freedom of navigation (FON) operations* Operations of *naval diplomacy* designed to challenge an attempt to restrict free

use of the seas by the passage of combat forces. FON operations may be *symbolic* or *coercive*.

***Friction*** Features of war that resist all action, make the simple difficult, and the difficult seemingly impossible. Friction
may be mental (such as indecision) or physical (such as
enemy fire). It may be externally imposed by enemy action,
geography or the weather, or self induced through a poor
plan or clash of personalities (ADP Vol 1). The expression
was used by Clausewitz in On War.

***Full command*** The military authority and responsibility of a
superior officer to issue orders to subordinates. It covers
every aspect of military operations and *administration* and
exists only within national Services (JSP 110). In the UK full
command is exercised by the single Service commanders
(eg CINCFLEET) who report to the United Kingdom Government through the Chief of the Defence Staff. See
*administrative authority*.

***Functional organization*** Command organization for maritime
forces reflecting the functions, missions or tasks of the
component elements. See *type organization*.

# G

***General war*** *War* involving all the resources of a nation. *Total
war* is general war waged towards unlimited objectives.

***Goal*** An expression of broad meaning embracing *aim,
mission, objective*, and purpose.

***Grand strategic level*** The level of command and planning for
armed conflict (*level of war*) at which all national resources
(diplomatic, economic, military, political, informational
and technological) are applied to achieve national security
policy objectives.

***Guerre de course*** A campaign consisting of attacks on enemy
shipping.

***Gunboat diplomacy*** Colloquial expression for *naval diplomacy*.

# H

*Handling Point 1 (HP1)* United Kingdom Logistics Start Point (such as a Naval Base, Royal Logistics Corps base, RAF Transport Command Air Station or UK commercial port).

*Harmonization (of ROE)* The process whereby the rules of engagement of more than one nation taking part in a multi-national operation are compared and altered where possible to achieve similar levels of permission and prohibition through the various national systems.

*High Seas* All parts of the sea which are not included in the *territorial seas* or *internal waters* of States. All States have the freedom to navigate or conduct other activities, subject to certain restrictions, on the high seas.

*Holding area* Area of sea occupied by surface forces with a stationary speed of advance.

*Holding operation* See *economy of force operation.*

*Horizontal escalation* Escalation by extension of combat into new geographic areas or environments.

*Host Nation Support (HNS)* Civil and military assistance rendered in peace and war by a host nation to allied forces and NATO organizations which are located on or in transit through the host nation's territory. (AJP1(A))

*Hostilities* Period between the onset of regular *combat* between parties and any cease fire or truce.

# I

*Immediate Reaction Forces (IRF)* NATO forces held routinely at the highest readiness. The *Standing Naval Forces* are maritime IRF.

*Infiltration* The covert movement of forces through or between defended areas to seize objectives in the enemy's rear.

***Influence over the Battlespace*** One of the *operational functions*. It describes the moulding of the situation in and around the operating area in order to prevent enemy action from *disrupting* the operation. Influence is achieved by a combination of *command and control warfare*, control of the electromagnetic spectrum, *interdiction* of enemy forces, and a responsive and agile force capable of acting faster than the enemy.

***Innocent passage*** Defined as navigation through the *territorial sea* of a State for the purpose of either traversing that sea without entering *internal waters*, or of proceeding in either direction between the high seas and internal waters. Vessels have the right to take innocent passage through *territorial seas* without interference by the coastal States concerned.

***Insurgency*** The actions of a minority group within a state intent on forcing political change by means of a mixture of subversion, propaganda and military pressure, aiming to persuade or intimidate the broad mass of the people to accept such change. (ADP Vol 1)

***Integrated Military Structure (IMS)*** See *NATO Integrated Military Structure (NIMS)*.

***Integrated multinational operation*** Operation in which forces of two or more nations operate under a *unified* command structure. Only integrated operations are truly *combined*.

***Interdiction*** An operation conducted to destroy, disrupt, neutralize or delay the enemy's military potential before it can be brought to bear effectively against friendly forces.

***Internal conflict*** Situation in which *violence* is threatened or used within a state's borders between competing groups for political reasons beyond levels that might be controlled by levels of civilian policing that are normal for that state.

***Internal Waters*** All waters actually within the territory of a State such as harbours, rivers and lakes; together with all other waters to landward of the baseline from which the State's *territorial sea* is measured. They are an integral part of the territory of the State and in them the laws of the land are supreme.

**International Strait** Considered to be a route which is used for international navigation which either connects one part of the *high seas* with another, or passes between one part of the high seas and the *territorial sea* of a State. Where there is no similarly convenient alternative route, the United Kingdom recognizes certain rights including unimpeded passage through international straits even where these pass through States' territorial seas.

**Interoperability** The ability of systems, units or forces to provide services to and accept services from other systems, units or forces and to use these services so exchanged to enable them to operate effectively together. (JSP 110)

**Intervention** *Campaign* or *operation* with limited objectives involving the entry of combat forces into the territory and territorial seas of another nation either with or without invitation.

# J

**Joint** *Activities*, operations, organizations etc in which elements of more than one Service of the same nation participate. (JSP 110)

**Joint Commander (JC)** In the United Kingdom command system a commander appointed by the Chief of Defence Staff to mount and sustain a joint operation and to exercise OPCOM of all the forces assigned to the operation. (JSP 1)

**Joint Force Air Component Commander (JFACC)** The JFACC is responsible for planning, co-ordination and tasking of air missions to meet the *Commander Allied Joint Forces' (COMAJF')* objectives. [AJP1(A)]. In national terms he would be responsible to the JFC.

**Joint Force Commander (JFC)** In the United Kingdom command system a commander appointed to employ a joint force in theatre and to exercise *OPCON* of that force. (JSP 1)

***Joint Force Headquarters (JFHQ)*** The operational headquarters of the *Joint Force Commander*, normally close to or within the theatre of operations. (JSP 1)

***Joint Headquarters (JHQ)*** The operational headquarters of the *Joint Commander*.

***Joint Theatre Plans*** National and NATO contingency plans for certain crisis operations, such as *Non-combatant Evacuation Operations*, in various parts of the world.

# L

***Land attack missile*** Submarine, surface ship, or naval air launched missile capable of engaging land targets.

***Layered defence*** The disposition of protective assets possessing a mixture of anti-submarine, anti- surface and anti-air capabilities in layers of screens and patrol areas about units of high value or crucial waters.

***LCAC*** Landing Craft Air Cushion (STANAG 1166)

***Levels of War*** The *grand strategic, military strategic, operational* and *tactical* levels of command and planning for armed conflict.

***Leverage*** (military) Disproportionate strategic or operational advantage gained by the use of a form of military power to exploit its geographical circumstances.

***Lift*** The capability to move resources between two points.

***Limited war*** *War* waged towards limited *war aims.*

***Linear operation*** Operation planned to proceed along a physical *line of operation.*

***Lines of communications (LOC)*** All the land, water and air routes that connect an operating military force with one or more bases of operations and along which supplies and reinforcements move (JSP110). See *line of support,* and *sea* *lines of communications (SLOC).*

**Line of operation**
1. (US Army) A directional orientation that connects the force with its base of operations and its objective. (FM 100-5)
2. (UK Army) Lines of operation describe how military force is applied in time and space through *decisive points* on the path to the *centre of gravity.* (ADP Vol 1)

**Line of support** A route (sea, land and air) that connects an operating military force with a logistics base and along which supplies move.

**Littoral region** The area from the open ocean to the shore which must be controlled to support operations ashore, and the area inland from shore that can be supported and defended directly from the sea.

**Lodgement Area** Following the invasion of a hostile coast and the establishment of a bridgehead ashore, the operations of invading forces are directed to the seizure of a lodgement area. This is an area which comprises adequate port, airfield and communications facilities and sufficient space for the assembly and maintenance of the total forces destined to take part in the campaign. (JSP110)

**Logistics** The science of planning and carrying out the movement and maintenance of forces. In its most comprehensive sense, these aspects of military operations which deal with:
• design and development, acquisition, storage, movement, distribution, maintenance, evacuation and disposition of material;
• movement, evacuation and hospitalization of personnel;
• acquisition or construction, maintenance, operation and disposition of facilities; and
• acquisition or furnishing of services. (JSP 110).

**LPD** Amphibious Transport, Dock (STANAG 1166) or Landing Platform Dock (JSP1).

**LPH** Amphibious Assault Ship, Helicopter (STANAG 1166) or Landing Platform Helicopter(JSP1).

**LSL** Landing Ship Logistic (STANAG 1166).

# M

**Main Defence Forces (MDF)** Forces assigned to NATO to enhance Reaction Forces and provide for the territorial defence of the alliance.

**Main effort** At the *operational level* an operation or other activity within a campaign into which an operational commander plans to concentrate his *combat power* usually to bring about a favourable *decisive event*. See *economy of force* and *holding operations*.

**Major NATO Commander (MNC)** The highest level of NATO military command beneath the Military Committee. The two MNCs are the Supreme Allied Commander, Europe (SACEUR), and the Supreme Allied Commander, Atlantic (SACLANT).

**Major Subordinate Commander (MSC)** Level of NATO military command directly subordinate to a *Major NATO Commander*. The Commander-in-Chief Eastern Atlantic Area (CINCEASTLANT) whose headquarters is at Northwood, Middlesex, is a MSC.

**Maldeployment** Force posture that is strategically or operationally disadvantageous in the pertaining circumstances.

**Manoeuvre** The employment of force on the battlefield through movement in combination with fire, or fire potential, to achieve a position of advantage in respect to the enemy in order to accomplish the mission. (JSP 110)

**Manoeuvre from the sea** The use of naval forces to contribute to *manoeuvre* ashore.

**Manoeuvre Warfare** A style of warfare that seeks to collapse an enemy's cohesion and effectiveness through a series of rapid, violent and unexpected actions that create a turbulent and rapidly deteriorating situation with which he cannot cope (US NDP1). Capital initial letters are used in this publication to distinguish *Manoeuvre Warfare* from *manoeuvre* above.

***Maritime campaign*** A connected series of operations conducted essentially by maritime forces including surface, subsurface, air forces and amphibious troops, for the purpose of gaining, extending, or maintaining control of the sea or of power projection.

***Maritime Component Commander*** The Maritime Component Commander is an officer subordinate to the Joint Force Commander responsible for maritime operational advice to him and the tactical employment of assigned *maritime forces.* See *Component Commander.*

***Maritime Domain*** The series of jurisdictional zones that surrounds the coast of a state. It includes territorial seas and the *Exclusive Economic Zone.*

***Maritime exclusion zone*** Declaration by a state of sea areas, including parts of the *high seas* in which conditions are imposed on ships and aircraft.

***Maritime forces*** Forces whose primary purpose is to conduct military operations at and from the sea. The expression includes warships and submarines, *auxiliaries, Ships Taken Up From Trade, organic* aircraft, fixed seabed installations, fixed shore installations (such as batteries) for the defence of seaways, shore based maritime aircraft and other shore based aircraft permanently assigned to maritime tasks.

***Maritime power projection (MPP)*** The use of seaborne military forces to influence events on land directly.

***Maritime superiority*** The capability of a state to establish *sea control* at will in any area of importance to that state.

***Materiel*** The stores and equipment (as opposed to personnel) available or required for an undertaking. (OED)

*Mexeflote* Large, powered pontoon capable of offloading heavy stores from amphibious shipping, *Ships Taken Up From Trade* and *RO-RO* ferries.

*Military Aid to Civil Ministries (MACM)* The use of military forces for non-military government tasks, including assistance to maintain the essentials of life in the community or to undertake urgent work of national importance. (SDE 93)

*Military Aid to the Civil Power (MACP)* Aid provided by the Armed Forces in the United Kingdom and the Dependent Territories for the direct maintenance or restoration of law and order in situations beyond the capacity of the civil power to resolve in any other way. (SDE 93)

*Military application (or use) of force* Applications of armed force in which *combat* is used or threatened, or in which combat potential is a prerequisite for success.

*Military Assistance*

1. Training, advice and other forms of assistance rendered by a government through its military services to another government in the process of developing and/or improving the operational performance of its armed forces.

2. In the context of peace *support operations*, all forms of mandated military assistance rendered to a foreign civil authority including the supervision of a transfer of power, reforming security forces, and developing or supporting civil infrastructure facilities (AFM WP).

*Military Assistance to the Civil Community (MACC)* The provision of Service personnel and equipment, both in emergencies and in routine situations, to assist the community at large. The Armed Forces are only used when there are no alternatives available, either because of urgency or expertise. (SDE 93)

*Military condition* A description of the degree of *military control* in a theatre possessed by protagonists in the five *warfare environments* of land, sea, air, space and the electronic spectrum. A primary planning task of an *operational commander* during *hostilities* is to define the military conditions that will achieve his given strategic *objectives*.

***Military containment*** See *containment*.

***Military exclusion zone (MEZ)*** Geographical (usually maritime) area including parts of the high seas within which a government states its intention to enforce the exclusion of all military units of a designated nation or nations or other grouping, using force if necessary. See *maritime exclusion zone* and *total exclusion zone (TEZ)*.

***Military force in support of diplomacy*** (Use of) Tasks in which military force is used to influence the policy of another government or quasi-governmental organization (such as the leadership of a civil war faction) directly. These tasks include reassurance and *coercion* (*deterrence* and *compellance*).

***Military strategic level*** The level of command and planning for armed conflict (*level of war*) at which military resources are applied to achieve policy objectives.

***Military strategy*** That component of national or multinational strategy, presenting the manner in which military power should be developed and applied to achieve national objectives or those of a group of nations (JSP 110)

***Military Tasks (MT)*** Formally defined activities of the Armed Forces of the United Kingdom for which there is a common Defence Policy rationale. They are grouped under the three *Defence Roles* and were first published in *Statement of Defence Estimates* 1993. Initial capital letters are used in this publication to distinguish these formal Military Tasks from any other task of military forces in the usual sense.

***Military use of force*** See *military (or combat governed) application of force*.

***Mission*** A clear, concise statement of the task of the command and its purpose. (JSP 110)

***Mission orders*** A style of orders to subordinate commanders that specify what is to be achieved without constraining the subordinate as to how it is to be achieved.

***Mobility*** A quality or capability of military forces which permits them to move from place to place while retaining the ability to fulfil their primary mission. (JSP 110)

***Multinational Logistic Support Commander (MNLC)*** Assigned by the lead *Major NATO Commander (MNC)* for a NATO operation. The MNLC and staff plan, coordinate and control, based on NATO Military Authorities' and national prearranged agreement, all maritime *logistic* shore support for *Multinational NATO Maritime Forces (MNMF)*. Additionally he will assume responsibility for all shuttle ships not under the control of the MNMF commander. The MNLC will report to the NATO Commander having *operational control (OPCON)* of the MNMF. (NATO)

***Multinational NATO Maritime Forces (MNMF)*** Multinational NATO *Reaction Forces* consisting of *Standing Naval Forces, NATO Task Groups, NATO Task Forces* and *NATO Expanded Task Forces.*

# N

***National Contingency Forces (NCF)*** United Kingdom *contingency forces* provided as *Military Tasks* under *Defence Role 3* to support the UK's wider security interests in the promotion of peace and stability. NCF also have uses under Defence Role 1.

***NATO Expanded Task Force (NETF)*** A force consisting of the elements of *NATO Task Forces* with multiple carriers, amphibious ships/landing forces and an enhanced complement of multi-mission capable escorts and submarines. It is a fully battle-capable force with a significant *maritime power projection* capability.

***NATO Integrated Military Structure (NIMS)*** The Integrated Military Structure of NATO comprises the NATO Military Command Structure (Including the Defence Planning

Committee, Military Committee, *Major NATO Commanders (MNCs)* and subordinate commands), the associated command boundaries, the Integrated Military Staffs at NATO Headquarters and those of subordinate commands), the Defence Planning System, the NATO Force Structure and NATO Infrastructure Programme.

**NATO Task Force (NTF)** A force consisting of the elements of a *NATO Task Group (NTG)* with amphibious ships/landing forces and a carrier, or both, to provide *control of the air* and limited *maritime power projection*.

**NATO Task Group (NTG)** A *task group* of one or more cruisers, and destroyers and frigates with submarines, maritime patrol aircraft and mine countermeasures forces as required.

**Naval Control of Shipping (NCS)** Control exercised by naval authorities of movement, routeing, reporting, convoy organization and tactical diversion of allied merchant shipping. It does not include the employment or active protection of such shipping (JSP 110).

**Naval diplomacy** The use of naval force in support of diplomacy to support, persuade, *deter* or *compel*.

**Naval forces** Seaborne military forces including warships, submarines, amphibious forces, *organic* aircraft and *auxiliaries*.

**Naval gunfire support (NGS)** Support to land operations from seaborne artillery.

**Naval Service(s)** The *Naval Service* is the Royal Navy, Royal Marines, Queen Alexandra's Royal Naval Nursing Service, their respective Reserves, the *Royal Fleet Auxiliary*, the Royal Maritime Auxiliary Services and members of the Civil Service under the direct management of the Navy Board. The United Kingdom *Naval Services* are the Naval Service and the Merchant Navy.

**No fly zone** Zone of airspace established by international mandate (or conceivably unilaterally as a *military* or *total* *exclusion zone*) in which the flying of specified types of aircraft is forbidden.

***Non-combatant Evacuation Operations (NEO)*** Operations involving the removal of UK nationals, and others if requested, from foreign territory using military forces to carry out that removal.

# O

***Objective*** An unambiguously defined purpose. The expression is often used figuratively to mean the physical *military condition* that will fulfil an objective (such as a location to be seized). See *aim* and *mission*.

***Offensive air support (OAS)*** OAS comprises *battlefield air interdiction (BAI)* and *close air support (CAS)*.

***Offensive operations*** Operations in which forces seek out the enemy in order to attack him. (JSP 110)

***Operation*** A military action or the carrying out of a strategic, tactical, service, training, or administrative military mission; the process of carrying on combat, including movement, supply, attack, defence and manoeuvre needed to gain the objectives of any battle or campaign. [AJP1(A)].

***Operational art*** The skilful employment of military forces to attain strategic *goals* through the design, organization, integration and conduct of campaigns and major operations (ADP Vol1). It is the essence of admiralship and generalship.

***Operational command (OPCOM)*** The authority granted to a commander to assign *missions* or tasks to subordinate commanders, to deploy units, to reassign forces and to retain or delegate *operational* and/or *tactical control* as may be deemed necessary. It does not of itself include responsibility for *administration or logistics*. (JSP 110). This is usually exercised by a national Single Service or *joint* commander of Flag or equivalent rank (eg CINCFLEET) and is the highest degree of command authority that nations will delegate to a *Major NATO Commander (MNC)*.

**Operational commander** A commander exercising command at the *operational level*.

**Operational control (OPCON)** The authority delegated to a commander to direct forces assigned so that the commander may accomplish specific *missions* or tasks which are usually limited by function, time or location; to deploy units concerned, and to retain or assign tactical control of those units. It does not include authority to assign separate employment of components of the units concerned. Neither does it of itself include *administrative* or *logistic* control. (JSP 110)

**Operational function** To maximize success an operational commander and his staff should group and focus planning effort to address certain key aspects of a campaign or major operation and subsequently monitor and review their execution closely. These aspects, the operational functions, are *command and control (C2)*, intelligence and *surveillance*, protection, *combat power, logistics,* and *influence over the battlespace.*

**Operational Level** The level of command and planning for military operations (*level of war*) at which *campaigns* and major operations are planned, conducted, and sustained to accomplish strategic objectives within theatres or areas of operation. (JSP 1)

**Operational pause** A periodic pause in operations while initiative is retained in other ways. Operational pauses may be required because a force has temporarily reached the end of its *sustainability*; because forces are exhausted; because of terrain or weather; because the character of the *campaign* has changed; [for political reasons]; or for a combination of these factors. (ADP Vol 1)

**Operational Sea Training (OST)** Training of individual naval units and groups of *maritime forces* in their operational roles and tasks under the supervision of a sea training authority and with the assistance of specialist training staff and facilities. See *work up*.

**Operational security (OPSEC)** The denial of operational information to the enemy.

**Operation other than war (OOTW)**
1. Operations carried out in situations of *conflict* other than *war*, either unilaterally or with allies or coalition partners, with the purpose of supporting the overall policy to resolve to terminate the conflict. OOTW include *peacekeeping, wider peacekeeping, peace enforcement, counter-insurgency operations* and limited *intervention* operations. (from ADP Vol 1)
2. Military activities during peacetime and *conflict* that do not necessarily involve armed clashes between ... organized forces. (FM100-5)

**Organic** In a naval context used to mean capabilities and resources that are borne within a *naval force* or formation. Often used of aircraft, *logistics*, weapons and sensors.

# P

**Partnership for Peace (PfP)** This initiative provides for non-NATO European nations who are members of the Organization for Security and Co-operation in Europe to become individual Partners of the Alliance. Each Partner agrees a specific programme with NATO Headquarters to meet its own needs and requirements. NATO will consult with a Partner who perceives a direct threat to its territorial integrity, political independence or security. Partners may participate in political and military bodies in NATO with respect to Partnership activities. They may take part in joint planning, joint military exercises and in creating an ability to operate with NATO forces in such fields as *peacekeeping*, search and rescue, humanitarian operations, and others as may be agreed.

***Peace building*** Identification and support of measures and structures which will solidify peace and build trust among former enemies,in order to avoid a relapse into *conflict.* [AJP1(A)]

***Peace enforcement*** Action including the use of military force on a multilateral basis to maintain or restore international peace previously agreed to by belligerents who may now be in *combat*, and to compel compliance with agreement to which parties have conferred or implied consent. Peace enforcement may entail the enforcement of *sanctions* and/ or direct military *intervention* to impose peace by the threat, or the actual use of force.

***Peace imposition*** Use of force to *compel* compliance with internationally expected patterns of behaviour, sanctions or resolutions, without any previously conferred or implied consent.

***Peacekeeping*** Measures by third parties to achieve and main-tain peace taken with impartiality and with the full consent of parties involved. See also *Wider Peacekeeping.*

***Peacemaking*** Diplomatic action to bring hostile parties to a negotiated agreement through peaceful means. (from AJP1(A)

***Peace support operations*** Generic term for *Peacemaking, Peace-keeping, Peace Building,* and *Peace Enforcement operations.* See also *Wider Peacekeeping.*

***Phase*** A period of a *sequential campaign* or major operation during which a large number of forces are involved in simi-lar activities (such as deployment). A transition to another phase, such as a shift from deployment to *defensive opera-tions,* indicates a shift in emphasis.

***Piracy*** The attack and robbery of merchant shipping and its cargo on the *high seas* by non-governmental forces.

***Poise*** An attribute of a *maritime force* which permits it to remain in international waters for long periods while retaining the ability to become engaged in events ashore or withdraw without risk of *embroilment*.

**Policing** See *constabulary applications*.

**Power projection** See *maritime power projection (MPP)*.

**Precursor operation** An *advance operation* to eliminate enemy sea denial forces such as conventional submarines, fast attack craft and mines from the path of the main force, a *holding area* or *amphibious objective area (AOA)*.

**Presence** The exercise of *naval diplomacy* in a general way involving deployments, port visits, exercising and routine operating in areas of interest to declare interest, reassure friends and allies and to *deter*.

**Preventive deployment** Deployment of forces to contribute to the prevention of development of a specific *crisis* or *conflict* generally.

**Principal Subordinate Commander (PSC)** The third level of NATO military command directly subordinate to a *Major Subordinate Commander*.

**Principles of War** Broad precepts distilled from experience which influence the conduct of armed conflict and which should inform all strategic and operational decisions. There is some variation between the Principles of War accepted by different nations. The United Kingdom Principles are at Annex A.

**Proactive** Action that seeks to preempt and control rather than respond to events by seizing and maintaining the initiative. The antithesis of "reactive".

**Prolongation** The deliberate extension of the length of a *conflict* as a means of outlasting or wearing down an enemy, or to provide an opportunity for new allies or reinforcements to be brought to bear. It can be considered as a form of *escalation*.

**Psychological operations (PSYOPS)** Activities carried out in peace and conflict which can be directed at friendly, enemy and neutral audiences. Their purpose is to influence attitudes and behaviour. In conflict PSYOPS seek to undermine an enemy's will,to fight, strengthen the support of the loyal and gain the support of the uncommitted. (ADP Vol 1)

# Q

**Qualitative escalation** *Escalation* between categories of warfare, for instance from conventional warfare to chemical and then to nuclear warfare.

**Quarantine** Expression used loosely to mean a restriction on the egress of certain types of cargo. Also used to mean embargo enforcement.

# R

**Raid** see *Amphibious raid*

**Rapid Reaction Forces (RRF)** NATO *Reaction Forces* at longer *readiness* than *Immediate Reaction Forces* and available to respond to a *crisis* which exceeds the capacity for IRF to *deter* or counter.

**Reach** The ability to operate for extended periods at considerable distance from shore support.

**Reaction Forces (RF)** Forces assigned to NATO and ready to respond at short notice to *crises* at various levels and, if necessary to contribute to initial defence. The categories of RF are *Immediate Reaction Forces* and *Rapid Reaction Forces.*

**Readiness** The time within which a unit or formation can be made ready at the appropriate location, that is its normal peacetime base or, for ships already at sea, its current location. A unit or formation is ready when it is prepared for its operational tasks at war establishments of personnel and equipment, trained for those tasks and supported by appropriate stocks. Ships and their *organic* air units will have the required *combat* load and other *logistic materiel* embarked or appropriately positioned. A Royal Marine formation will have the required weapons and equipment, as well as basic loads of supply, collocated or appropriately positioned.

**Rear operations** Land operations to increase freedom of action by protecting a force, sustaining combat operations and retaining freedom of manoeuvre of uncommitted forces. They include reception into theatre, assembly, movement and security of reserves; redeployment of forces out of contact with the enemy; *host nation support*; establishment and protection of bases and *lines of support* and support for and protection of civilians and civilian installations. (ADP Vol 1)

**Reconnaissance** The obtaining of information by visual observation or other detection methods about the activities and resources of an enemy, or data about meteorological, hydrographical or geographic characteristics. (AP 3000). See *surveillance*.

**Recognized Maritime Picture (RMP)** The fullest achievable agreed level of identification and tracking of all air, surface and sub-surface contacts in the area of interest. The RMP is normally associated with the Recognized Air Picture (RAP) of the same area.

**Reconstitution** The expansion of force structures and infrastructure beyond existing levels, including the raising of new units and formations and the expansion of industrial capacity to support the procurement of equipment and stocks. See *Regeneration*.

**Regional Naval Control of Shipping** Voluntary participation in *Naval Control of Shipping* by ship owners and operators within a clearly defined geographical region or regions.

**Regeneration** The timely activation, in full or in part, of existing force structures and infrastructure, including the restoration of manning, equipment and stocks to war levels. See *Reconstitution*.

**RO-RO ferries** Roll on - Roll Off ferries into and from which vehicles can be driven from and to a wharf or jetty.

***Roulement*** The rotation of units in the front line with those in reserve in order to maintain the fighting effectiveness of the forces engaged in an operation.

***Royal Fleet Auxiliary (RFA)*** The Royal Fleet Auxiliary (RFA) is a civilian manned flotilla owned and operated by the Ministry of Defence to provide *logistic* support for the armed services but primarily the Royal Navy.

***Rules of Engagement (ROE)*** Directives issued by competent military authority which specify the circumstances and limitations under which forces will initiate and/or continue combat engagement. UK ROE are expressed in permissions and prohibitions.

# S

***Sanction (United Nations)*** A penalty imposed on a state with the intention of influencing that state to comply with a Security Council Resolution or otherwise to abide by international law.

***Screening*** System of defence of a force or area using protective units deploying sensors and weapon systems in sectors or patrol areas around the force. See *layered defence*.

***Sea communications*** See *sea lines of communications (SLOC)*

***Sea control*** The condition that exists when one has freedom of action to use an area of sea for one's own purposes for a period of time and, if necessary, deny its use to an opponent. Sea control includes the airspace above the surface and the water volume and seabed below.

***Sea denial*** The condition short of full *sea control* that exists when an opponent is prevented from using an area of sea for his purposes

***Sealift*** The movement of resources between points by carriage in shipping.

***Sea lines of communications (SLOC)*** The sea routes that connect an operating military force with one or more bases of operations and along which supplies and reinforcements move (from JSP110). The expression is sometimes used more broadly in a strategic sense to include commercial shipping routes.

*Sequel* Subsequent operation based on the possible outcomes of the current operations. The execution of a sequel normally means beginning another *phase* of a *campaign*. A form of "what if?". (US FM 100-5)

*Sequencing* The arrangement of events in a *sequential campaign* in the order most likely to achieve the elimination of the enemy's *centre of gravity*. (ADP Vol 1)

*Sequential campaign* A campaign which consists of a series of discrete *phases*, steps or actions each of which is shaped to some extent on the outcome of those preceding.

*Services assisted evacuation (SAE)* *Non-combatant evacuation operation (NEO)* in which the host nation can guarantee the security of the evacuation and United Kingdom or coalition forces armed forces provide assistance to the process.

*Services protected evacuation (SPE)* *Non-combatant evacuation operation (NEO)* in which armed forces are required for the protection of the evacuees as well as providing an avenue of evacuation and transport.

*Shakedown* (colloquial) Period of basic sea or harbour training for naval units after a period without training or operational experience, or for a naval force on first assembling to build interopera-bility. Shakedown may be part of or precede *operational sea training* or it may be informal.

*Ships taken up from trade (STUFT)* Merchant ships chartered or requisitioned for maritime operations.

*Simultaneity* Element of campaign and operational design that seeks to disrupt the decision-making process of the enemy commander by confronting him with a number of problems simultaneously, such as attack or the threat of attack from several directions. He is denied the ability to concentrate on one problem at a time or establish priorities between problems.

**Spectrum of conflict** The full range of levels of *violence* from stable peace through *conflict* and the onset of combat to *limited war* and *general war*, and finally to strategic nuclear exchange. Often displayed graphically relating military tasks and types of operation to levels of violence, and sometimes also to probability of occurrence.

**Standing Naval Forces (SNF)** NATO's maritime multinational *Immediate Reaction Forces*. They are the Standing Naval Force Atlantic (STANAVFORLANT), Standing Naval Force Mediterranean (STANAVFORMED) and Standing Naval Force Channel (STANAVFORCHAN - which is shortly to be redesignated, Standing Naval Mine Countermeasures Force or STANAVMINFOR). The first two are principally frigate and destroyer formations. The third is a mine countermeasures force.

**Statement on the Defence Estimates (SDE)** Annual statement presented to Parliament by the Secretary of State for Defence which may include the public presentation of Defence Policy. Also known as the Defence White Paper.

**Strategic air offensive** The use of airpower to strike directly and with precision at the enemy's strategic *centres of gravity* including leadership, military forces, infrastructure and research and production facilities. (AP3000)

**Strategic level** See *grand strategic* and *military strategic levels*.

**Strategic nuclear deterrence** Deterrence of aggression effected by the existence of long range nuclear weapons capable of holding at risk objects of value in the homeland of a any possible aggressor.

**STUFT** See *Ships Taken Up From Trade*.

**Suasion** See *armed suasion*.

**Sub-strategic nuclear deterrent capability** The capability to deliver more limited nuclear attacks than that maintained for *strategic nuclear deterrence* to provide nuclear deterrence in circumstances in which the threat of strategic nuclear attack may not be credible.

***Surveillance*** The systematic observation of the environments (sea, land, air, space and the electromagnetic spectrum) by visual, acoustic, electronic, photographic or other means (AP 3000). See reconnaissance.

***Survivability*** The ability of a ship to continue fighting when it has suffered damage.

***Sustainability*** The ability of a force to maintain the necessary level of combat power for the duration required to achieve its objectives (AAP-6). See *endurance.*

***Symbolic use of force*** A form of *naval diplomacy* in which naval forces can be used purely to signal a message to a specific government while not in themselves posing any threat to an opponent or providing significant military assistance to a friend.

***Synchronization*** The ability to focus resources and activities in time and space to produce maximum *combat power* to bring about a *decisive event. Synchronization* differs from *simultaneity* as the purpose is to achieve decisive coincidence of the effects of activities rather than the activities themselves.

***Systemic disruption*** Reduction by the selective use or threat of *combat* of the cohesion of an enemy force's total combat system to the extent that it is unable to deliver combat to achieve the military objectives required of it. See *disruption.*

# T

***Tactical command (TACOM)*** The authority delegated to a commander to assign tasks to forces under his command for the accomplishment of the *mission* assigned by higher authority. (JSP 110)

***Tactical control (TACON)*** The detailed, and usually, local direction and control of movements or manoeuvres necessary to accomplish *missions* or tasks assigned. (JSP 110)

***Tactical [level]*** The tactical level of warfare involves the direction of military resources to achieve operational objectives. (JSP 1)

***Task element (TE)*** The fourth and lowest level of *echelonment* in a *task organization*.

***Task force (TF)*** A [temporary] grouping of units, under one commander, formed for the purpose of carrying out a specific operation or *mission* (JSP 110). In a *functional* or *task organization* a TF is the highest level of *echelonment*. See *battleforce*.

***Task group (TG)*** A [temporary] grouping of units under one commander subordinate to a *task force* commander, formed for the purpose of carrying out a specific function or functions. The second highest level of *echelonment* in a *task organization*. See *battlegroup*.

***Task organization*** *Functional* command *organization* in which the component units and formations are organized according to task into *task forces*, *task groups*, *task units* and *task elements*.

***Task unit (TU)*** The third level of *echelonment* in a task *organization*.

***Tempo*** The rate or rhythm of military activity relative to the enemy, within tactical engagements and battles and between major operations.

***Territorial Sea*** The territorial sea of a State consists of a belt of water adjacent to the coast of the State and extending up to a maximum distance of 12 nautical miles to the seaward of the baselines drawn in accordance with the accepted principles of international law. It forms part of the sovereign territory of the state and is under that State's control and jurisdiction.

***Total exclusion zone (TEZ)*** Maritime geographical area including parts of the *high seas* within which a government states its intention to enforce the exclusion of all ships and aircraft, both military and civilian. of a designated nation or nations or other grouping, using force if necessary. See *maritime exclusion zone* and *military exclusion zone (MEZ)*.

***Total war*** *General war* waged towards unlimited objectives.

***Turning movement*** A form of *manoeuvre* in which an attacker secures key terrain in an enemy's rear forcing him to abandon his prepared defence and attack in an undesirable direction and at a time of his opponent's choice. (US FM 100-5)

***Type organization*** Command organization of *naval forces* by type or class of unit normally used for *administrative* purposes. See *functional organization*.

# U

***Unified*** Forces under the command or control of a single commander. A command that includes forces from different Services and/or nations. An imprecise expression variously meaning *joint*, *combined*, and *integrated*.

# V

***Versatility*** The ability to change fighting posture quickly without recourse to outside resources.

***Vertical escalation*** An increase in intensity of *combat* during *hostilities*. It is sometimes understood to include *qualitative escalation*.

***Violence*** Conduct involving the use of great physical force. In the military context violence may result in .injury 'and damage to or destruction of resources.

# W

*War* A sustained period during which two or more nations, alliances, coalitions, or factions within nations attempt to achieve mutually exclusive objectives by the use and threat of regular and sustained *combat*. The expression is normally associated with combat at high levels of intensity but criteria of intensity would exclude some *civil* and guerilla wars. Whether or not a state of war exists is very much in the perception of the parties involved. One party may believe that it is at war, for instance a group of *insurgents*, while the other party, in this case a government, may consider that it faces a problem of peace disorder. To Thomas Hobbes (Leviathan) the relationship between combat and war is that of a shower to bad weather. *Hostilities* is a more precise expression for any period between the onset of regular combat between parties and any cease-fire or truce. See *general war, limited war, civil war,* and *operations other than war (OOTW)*.

*War aim* The *grand strategic* or political aim of a government or faction on outbreak of *war* and during its conduct and termination phases. *War aims* are loosely used to mean grand strategic *objectives* generally that are being pursued during *hostilities*.

*Warfare environment* The five warfare environments are sea, land, air, space and the electromagnetic spectrum.

*Wider Peacekeeping* Aspects of *peacekeeping* operations, other than *observer missions* and *interposition*, carried out with the consent of the belligerent parties but in an environment that may be highly volatile. Wider peacekeeping includes *conflict prevention, demobilization operations, military assistance,* humanitarian relief and the guarantee and denial of movement.

*Withdrawal* See *Amphibious withdrawal*.

*Work up* Colloquial expression for *operational sea training*. It is also used for a period of informal sea training.

# Further Reading

K BOOTH **Navies and Foreign Policy**
London, Croom Helm, 1977

SIR JAMES CABLE **Gunboat Diplomacy 1919 - 1991 (Third Edition)**
Basingstoke, Macmillan, 1994

SIR JULIAN CORBETT **Some Principles of Maritime Strategy**
*With an introduction and notes by Eric Grove,*
London: Brassey's (UK) Ltd 1988

COLIN S GRAY **The Leverage of Sea Power**
New York: The Free Press imprint of Simon and Schuster, 1992

ERIC GROVE **The Future of Seapower**
London: Routledge 1990

Ed. J HATTENDORF **Mahan on Naval Strategy**
*Selected excerpts from the writings of Rear Admiral Alfred Thayer Mahan USN with a commentary*
Annapolis MD USA: Naval Institute Press, 1991.

REAR ADMIRAL J R HILL **Maritime Strategy for Medium Powers**
London, Croom Helm, 1986

EDWARD N LUTTWAK **The Political Uses of Sea Power**
Baltimore MD, Johns Hopkins University Press, 1974

HERBERT ROSINSKI **The Development of Naval Thought**
Newport RI USA, Naval War College Press, 1977

CAPTAIN S W ROSKILL RN **The Strategy of Sea Power**
London, Collins, 1972

GEOFFEY TILL **Maritime Strategy in the Nuclear Age (Second Edition)**
London Macmillan, 1984

REAR ADMIRAL J C WYLIE USN **Military Strategy**
Annapolis MD USA Naval Institute Press, 1989

M C PUGH *(Editor)* **Maritime Security and Peacekeeping**
*A framework for United Nation Operations,*
Manchester UNiversity Press, 1994

# Index

Innocent passage 51, 218
Insurgency 44, 112, 218
Integrated Military Structure (IMS)
    *see* NATO Integrated Military
    Structure (NIMS)
Integrated multinational operation
    131, 218
Integration,
    degrees of 161;
    full or combination 133
Intelligence 62, 86, 117, 136, 138,
    162, 163, 229;
    operational 118;
    strategic 117-18
Intentions 136
Interdiction 83, 95, 166, 168, 218
internal,
    conflict 32, 218;
    waters 52, 122, 218
International law 51, 95, 102, 235
International Straits 51, 219
Interoperability 133, 219
Interpositions 241
Intervention 43, 70, 92, 171, 219, 230
Iterative,
    planning 124-5;
    process 110

Joint 14, 69, 201, 228;
    activities 219;
    attributes 61-2;
    campaign 86, 189;
    expeditionary force 56
Joint Commander (JC) 108, 130, 219
Joint Force Air Component
    Commander (JFACC) 170, 219
Joint Force Commander (JFC) 108,
    130, 149, 173, 207, 219-20
Joint Force Headquarters (JFHQ)
    173, 220
Joint Headquarters (JHQ) 130, 190,
    220
Joint Operationa Logistics Pipeline
    193
Joint Theatre Plans 87, 220
JSP 1 14
judgement 139

Korean War 75
Kuwait 21

Land attack missiles 86, 170, 174, 220
Land attack in support of sea control
    86
Land doctrine 110
Land Force Commander 190
Land warfare, significance of 71-2
Landing Craft Air Cushion (LCAC)
    174-5, 220
Landing Force 169, 175
Landing Platform Dock (LPD) 174
Landing Platform Helicopter (LPH)
    173, 174
Landing Ships Logistic (LSL) 174
Layered defence 78, 97, 166; *see also*
    screening
Leadership 119, 178-9;
    effective 138-9, 142;
    qualities for 140-1
Level of war 42-3, 47, 73, 198, 216,
    225, 229;
    *see also* grand strategic level;
    military strategic level;
    operational level
Levels of command 130, 190; national
    143
Leverage 60-1, 84, 125, 165, 220
Liaison 131, 165
Life at sea 178-9
Life cycle 63
Lift 59-60, 60, 86, 174, 220
Limited war 43, 220, 237
Linear operations 115, 220
Lines of communication (LOC) 220;
    *see also* line of support; sea lines of
    communication (SLOC)
Lines of operation 71, 221
Lines of support 56, 71, 123, 149,
    168, 189, 195, 221, 234;
    land 147;
    sea 146, 168
Littoral region 50, 54, 56, 68, 69, 123,
    170, 221
Lodgement area 84, 170, 194, 221
Logistic,

Printed in the United Kingdom for HMSO
Dd 301631 C125 11/95 9385 3318